Kenwanna W

Grandpa's Pound Cake

formally titled
Scared and Pregnant

Grandpa's Pound Cake
Copyright © 2018 Kenwanna Wheat
All rights reserved.
Grandpa's Pound Cake ISBN: 978-0692125744
formally titled
Scared and Pregnant ISBN: 9798663007818

DEDICATION

I dedicate this novel to my mother, Stepfather A. Brown, sister, grandparents, Aunt Sandra, and my two children. All these people are special to me, and bits and pieces of them are a part of the recipe that makes me the woman, mother, daughter, niece, granddaughter, and sister that I am – my version of pound cake. I would like to thank Ebony, Sandra, and Chelahnnhe! I appreciate all of you! A special thanks to my friends that believed in me and inspired me to keep writing. You know who you are. I appreciate the motivation. It has meant the world to me and helped keep this book alive.

CONTENTS

1. SELF-FULFILLING PROPHECY
2. LIFE CHANGING JOURNEY
3. THE HOSPITAL
4. ONE WEEK LATER IN DH
5. UNLOCKING PRIVACY
6. GRANDPA'S POUND CAKE
7. GRADUATION CEREMONY
8. MY SISTER THE LEGEND
9. SPADES TOURNAMENT
10. PERSPECTIVE
11. EUPHRASIA
12. CAGED BIRDS DO SING
13. BIRTH OF MY LITTLE ANGEL
14. GRANDMA
15. LOSING IT
16. JAILED BIRDS DO FLY

Grandpa's Pound Cake

1. SELF-FULFILLED PROPHECY

I woke up feeling like I was on life support. I was one drop away from dying from dehydration. I looked like cactus braving the cold Ohio winters, crumbled up, wrinkled, and weak. Ohio wintertime was tough on the cactus, much like, pregnancy was tough on me. In Ohio, cactus thrived in the summertime, however; in the wintertime, cactus fell flattened to the ground under the wintry conditions. I felt and looked like dying cactus.

I leaned over the side of my bed, lifted the trashcan close to my face, and threw up. About a month ago, I found out I was three months pregnant. I laid in bed and struggled to sit up. My equilibrium was shaky from the imbalance of my hormones.

By the time I figured out I was pregnant, my ribs and cheekbones protruded through my skin like thin elastic. My health declined more by each passing day.

I lost a half a pound a day. I felt my energy supply depleting. For over three months, every morning brought on terrifying anxiety of repeating the previous day. With each morning, I confronted the challenge and found ways to replenish and nourish my body to survive. Being afflicted with Hyperemesis Gravidarum was a severe pregnancy condition that some pregnant women get. There is no effective protocol that exists to treat the condition.

At the beginning of my pregnancy, my throat, my stomach, bladder, and brain functioned like a broke down automobile. My head and body hurt; and my body rejected food and water. I couldn't swallow my saliva and I spat and vomited multiple times throughout the day. After sipping a drop of water, I'd throw up a gallon of bodily fluids. I stopped peeing, pooping, and sleeping. I was exhausted, dehydrated, and my potassium levels were low. The baby growing inside of me felt more like a parasite than a human being.

My body was under attack, and I was losing the battle. I was no longer myself; I was no longer Keturah. It was my senior year of high school, and I managed to go to school when I felt well enough to make it through the day. I had already passed the first three semesters and knew I had the grades to graduate whether I went to school or not. I wasn't worried about graduating. I stopped hanging out with my boyfriend and my friends. I didn't look or act like me. I was not Keturah Black. I was outside of myself.

My body got weaker daily and I had dropped over twenty-five pounds. Time moved slower every day. Seconds last for hours. My illness disrupted my vision, sense of smell, sense of feeling, and sense of touch. Beautiful visions and sounds of children smiling and laughing; birds chirping early in the morning; and, other pleasant sounds that usually brought an instant smile to my face were now displeasing to my ears.

The only part of my senses that worked was my sense of smell. I could smell everything and everybody. God forbid them from having a bad stomach or bad tooth - I could smell the rot from within them. Being pregnant is the only time I ever begged God to die. Through pregnancy, God gave me a glimpse of what it felt like to be dying. Moreover, with my near-death experience, boredom and isolation came along for the ride and slowed down every second of my life.

Besides me feeling terrible, it was the morning of my sentencing for stabbing my neighbor. I grabbed the trash bag out of the trashcan, stumbled downstairs, walked to the kitchen, and threw my puke away. I made my way to the bathroom and got in the shower. Showers made me feel better – in a way hydrating me like it would a flower.

"Keturah come on, I got to get in the shower too!" my mother yelled outside the bathroom door. She was always in a rush. With her breathing down my neck, I didn't have time to do much to my hair. I slapped some gel on my edges, brushed my hair up into a ponytail, placing it perfectly in the middle of my head.

For a moment, I saw myself as a famous hairstylist at the "Hair Wars" expected to perform hair miracles in five seconds flat. Last night, I rolled my weave on rollers and microwaved it. The hair was a little choppy because I'd already worn it before, however, I could still work with it. Over the years, I'd developed an interest in cosmetology. My hair was a top priority and I made sure my hair was stylish. Even if I got it done professionally, I went home and put my own spin on it.

My life and passion to make women look and feel phenomenal are possible due to my exposure to the works of important African American women innovators like Madame C. J. Walker and Christina Jenkins. Both phenomenal women developed various methods of hair care for black women. Like them, I often dreamt of becoming a woman that helps other women find the beauty they crave.

I took the rollers out and bobby pinned the two-toned, black, and wine-red weave to my natural ponytail. I could do all kinds of hairstyles with a couple of tracks of artificial hair. From sewing to gluing it in my hair, microwaving it, blue weave, purple weave, any color of weave - I made sure that it matched my outfit. Christina Jenkins would be impressed with the improved techniques and uses of her invention of hair weave.

My wardrobe was easier to put together because my mother was addicted to shopping. I put on my peach top with a matching long skirt, nude stockings, and brown flat shoes. I sat on my vanity chair, looked in the mirror, and pulled my curls apart. I sprayed and fused my hair until the curls were stuck in place. My hair looked like a queen's crown made of curls. Though my scalp was still wet, my hair was cute, and it would have to do. I didn't want to look too flashy or too urban. I intended to look cute and innocent.

"Why are we rushing?" I asked. "We don't have to be there until nine o'clock. I'm-ma throw-up again," I whined as I concentrated on holding in my puke.

"Did you eat some crackers?" my mother asked.

"No, I don't feel like eating. I'll get something off one of those food carts after court."

"I'm not sure if that's a good idea if you're not holding down fluids. At least try to drink some orange juice or something."

Going downtown and buying a sandwich off a food truck was one of my mother's rituals. I associate downtown Columbus with my mother treating me to a sandwich from one of those food trucks, seeing the fourth of July fireworks, and the holiday parades, as special occasions. I hoped the exciting feeling of downtown and the familiar smells of sausage, onions, and green peppers gave me an appetite. Over the last few days, my body began to feel slightly stronger. I ate and drank some, although, not on command.

My mother, her second husband Phil, and I got into the car and began our journey to the courthouse in silence. I drove down the streets of my mind that brought me to the present moment in time and my current situation. I was unaware that I had once again, walked into a situation that physically and mentally forced me to have an out-of-body experience.

As we sped down the highway, I looked out the window and noticed how fast the objects outside the window appeared to be moving. As we cruised at slower speeds, I noticed the blurry frames became more visible. As we exited the ramp of the highway and came to a complete stop at the red light, the blurry pictures blended into a series of frames and became one frame sharply focused. In those few seconds, I had time to look around and observe my surroundings. As we continued to cruise down the road, I noticed the car in the front of us frequently pressed on their breaks, for no other reason than to express their free will, which forced Phil to press his breaks.

I'd been on house arrest for over a year and found an analogy between my life and this car ride, which appeared to explain my current situation in a nutshell. Magistrate Bailey ordered me to house arrest, which forced me to slow down my life. Getting pregnant forced my life to come to a complete stop. The idea of house arrest and pregnancy was synonymous with the car riding in front of us. I imagined Magistrate Bailey, before whom I'd soon be standing, was the person driving the car in front of us. She was intentionally antagonizing me and forcing this ride to be longer than it had to be. I hoped and prayed she'd immediately increase her speed, which was my prayer that she would show me mercy during sentencing.

Sitting at the next stoplight, I looked at the car to the left of us. Four teenagers around my age were in the care laughing. At that moment, I wished that I was in that car. Before our car turned the corner, over the laughter that filled the car, I heard one of the teens say to the other, "You lie! You lie!"

I had an epiphany and recalled the night my best friend Ava and I went to see her friend Stacy. Hanging out that summer night, Stacy suggested we visit Mitch. He said Mitch had some weed. Our plan was to smoke-up Mitch's weed. It wasn't the first time we took advantage of him. Stacy was right, church boy Mitch was a little on the naïve side, but he usually had some killer weed.

As we sat in his car smoking and talking, I don't know what motivated me, but I started making up an elaborate lie. It was just a joke, all in good fun. At that time, I didn't know the power of my tongue or the life of the words birthed from it. The lie wasn't part of our plan, but Ava and Stacy went along with it. We had fun with the elaborate lie and my storytelling skills.

"I was born in jail," I added more details in my word choice.

"What did your mom do to go to jail?" Mitch asked.

"She almost killed an old boyfriend."

"Was it your dad?"

"No, it was some other nigga."

Mitch listened attentively asking questions along the way. I explained how I was born in jail and filled in the holes with my imagination of lies. The story sounded and felt real. I was surprisingly convincing. I'm not sure where those ideas came from, but remember Ava, Stacy, and me laughing after the fact. It's chilling how that story developed into some type of self-fulfilling prophecy because there I was pregnant and heading to the courthouse for sentencing.

I was familiar with courtrooms; this wasn't my first time in one. However, it was my first time being sentenced by a judge. On my previous visit to a courtroom, I was the victim and instructed not to look at the defendant – my rapist. My Aunt Harriet also instructed me not to use the word coochie.

Instead, she instructed me to say vagina. In the courtroom, I followed my attorney's advice and did not look at the defendant. However, I had never referred to my coochie as a vagina; of course, I got on the witness stand and called it a coochie. As a result, I learned the importance of teaching children the proper names for their body parts. My aunt probably had a heart attack. I felt different being the defendant and the one standing before the Judge for sentencing. Being the defendant was altogether different from being a victim.

"Keturah Black!" the guard called out. I trembled as my attorney escorted my parents and me, along with my shame through the courtroom doors. I walked down the aisle with both of my arms awkwardly stiff at my side. I didn't look around at anybody sitting in the room that day. I kept my eyes focused on Magistrate Bailey. But, before we got to our assigned seats, out the corner of my eye, I spotted Boomquifa and her family sitting at the table where plaintiffs sit. My parents and I stood on the other side of the courtroom quietly waiting for Magistrate Bailey to speak.

Magistrate Bailey began with words full of compassion and empathy regarding the childhood trauma that I had experienced. Most of what she said gave me hope. I waited for the climax of her summary because I wasn't sure where she was heading, as she continued with her long drawn out monologue of my biography.

"I sentence you to one year with a maximum of two years to the Ohio Department of Youth Services (O.D. Y.S)," she stated.

I stood there shocked. Before the utterance of those words, the hope that entered the courtroom with me quickly died. After I heard, "One to two years," I didn't hear anything. Her compassion and empathy quickly eroded as her words paralyzed my internal being.

Neither my mother nor my lawyer told me there was a possibility of me going to jail. I felt blindsided. I felt like the victim. I felt sorry for myself. As I stood there shocked, scared, extremely angry, and confused, I began hyperventilating. Snot and tears ran down my face as I stood in the courtroom in total disbelief.

I was sick and pregnant, graduation was weeks away, and I was sentenced to one to two years in a juvenile jail. I was in too many situations at the same time. I looked at my mother and wanted to throw my arms around her. Through some tough times in my life, I managed to survive without her. But this time was different. I needed my mother. I wanted and needed to hug her.

The guard walked over and led me to the holding room in the back of the courtroom. "Find a seat," the guard said.

I walked in the holding area, looked around,

spotted an empty seat, and sat down. My mother taught me to never let anyone see me cry. I fought hard to hold back my tears. However, the harder I tried not to cry, the more my tears exploded. That day, I had no choice but to make an exception, as I was unprepared for the emotional rollercoaster ride, I found myself riding. My tears caught up to the snot racing down my face. I cried uncontrollably.

Already irritated and annoyed when this nappy-headed boy, no more than 11 years old, stared me down and seductively licked his tongue at me.

"What the hell are you staring at?" I growled at him. I wanted to get up and smack the shit out of him for disrespecting me and not respecting the tragic moment I was having with myself.

"Don't bring that mess in here!" the guard warned pointing her finger at me with an intimidating tone and look of dominance in her eyes.

I sat there angry and scared. Though, I was angrier about having to sit there and be disrespected by the nappy-headed boy than for the guard redirecting me.

After the last inmate's hearing, the guard led me and two other girls one-way and another guard led the boys in another direction. We arrived at the girls' area and the guard led us to the showers. I didn't comprehend what was happening right away; the guard handed each of us a plastic bag and an orange jumpsuit.

"Undress and shower - you all need to wash your

hair thoroughly and change into the suit," the guard told us. "And make sure you take that ponytail out your head!" the guard pointed at me.

The guard nagged on and on. I was steaming mad. Being pissed off and mad is an understatement. "I just did my hair!" I thought loudly to myself. I wished the guard would shut up and let me soak in my sorrow in silence. My head was banging. I removed every piece of culture from my head to my toes and washed off the expensive moisturized soap and lotion I applied earlier that morning. Whatever moisture was in my skin, washed away with the soap provided by the jail, which felt harsh and dry. Everything that made me Keturah washed down the shower drain.

The guard walked us to the processing center, and I handed over my items to the guard at the counter. For the first time in my life, I had my fingerprints recorded. When I reached the female side of the facility, two yellow lines painted and split the middle of the floor met me where the hallway began and commanded my attention.

"Hands behind your back and stay on the line." The guard led the two girls and me to the cafeteria and we walked one behind the other on the yellow line. "Go through the line, grab a tray, and sit at a table."

I didn't know if the chili was good or if I was hungry, but I was able to keep some food down. "I'm not supposed to be here." Were the only words that echoed in my head, over, and over as I ate the chili. I had never imagined myself being in jail. My mind visited my short-term goals and drifted into a place where lost goals hid. My life was ruined. Here I was, only a couple hours into my sentence and I didn't think I'd make it another day. I thought I'd be on my way to college after high school. I never imagined I'd be in jail instead. I was literally, barefoot and pregnant. If my friends could see the plastic beige sandals I sported, not cute.

Raw Sewer

The next morning, I woke up with overwhelming anxiety. I felt myself grieving on the inside. It was silent and painful. The affliction in my stomach ached to my temples. The headache from the day before still afflicted me. Although I had a life growing inside me, I wanted to die. I wished I could sleep through the next year. Waking up pregnant was already a complicated process because of my spitting, mucus, and vomiting problem. Adding the four walls and small space made waking up a more devastating honor.

My tears leaked bits of sadness on my pillow. I wished that I was able to wake up in my bed. I wanted to throw-up in my toilet; I wanted to find my magical yellow brick road home. I didn't want this experience engraved on my tombstone. Being a juvenile felon was far from how I wanted my family, peers, the world, and unborn child to perceive me.

I worked for twelve years for a diploma and was only two weeks away from receiving it. I'd always dreamt of the day when I would walk across the stage amongst my peers, draped in my blue and gold cap and gown. It was my dream to lift my tassel to the left side while people cheered me on in the background. I wanted to look out in the crowd at my parents and wanted to hear them scream as loud as they were proud. Unfortunately, I turned on the ignition to life, only to graduate into an unfamiliar world of surprises.

When I stood in the courtroom, I never imagined my reality check would be so harsh. I was familiar with the highs and lows of life; because, from the time I was eight years old, every seven years something tragic happened. I got used to bad things happening that I often anticipated, waited, and braced myself for the occurrence of those experiences. This last event was confirmation that my theory about my life was true. I laid in my cell and choked off my saliva and the raw - rotten feces - urine stench seeping from the toilet. My senses were hypersensitive due to the side effects of my pregnancy. My nose was not a normal pregnancy nose; I had a heightened sense of smell due to my sickly condition.

All my senses suffered miserably and none of them worked properly. After I spent all night gagging with my stomach churning and churning, I gagged and regurgitated hot stomach acids stinging my throat, nose, and brain. My attempts to throw-up in the toilet failed more miserably. The smell was so violent that I created a pathway of puke in my attempts to make it to the toilet. I inhaled the revolting smell that churned my stomach, turning my vomiting into a hard cycle to stop once started.

It was around six o'clock in the morning. From where I was laying, I could see a partial piece of the moon through a small window. I heard the doors unlocking and opening one after the other and the sound moving closer to me. The guard opened my door and stepped into the four-walled sewer. She got a whiff of the rotten-feces, urine-stench, which must've filled her with repulsion. She became my hero.

"How long you been in here?" the guard asked with concern.

"Since yesterday," I answered. I was happy she cared, my eye ducts began to swell with tears, but I was able to restrain them by taking in a deep breath of the contaminated air.

"Pull your mattress out here. Whoever put you in here know they had no business doing it! They wouldn't want their child in this filth!"

I was relieved. The smell of the cell was unbearable. I thought the vile treatment was inhumane but normal treatment for jailbirds – sadly, I didn't know any better. The urine and feces left to marinate in the toilet for days eventually turned into a mix of toxic waste filling the cell with the thick fumes. The guards turned the toilet off because some girl intentionally clogged it up; and, for some crazy reason, the last guard showed me no mercy or human decency and thought it was okay to leave my pregnant nose to endure the painful smell. Who knows how many fumes I ingested? Yuck!

Hours later, the guard opened the doors of the other girls. The nurse called the girls on meds to the pod door. I was surprised to hear my name called. I walked to the pod door and there stood the nurse with a cart of medication. The nurse must've noticed the puzzling look on my face because she handed me a small cup and said, "Here's your prenatal vitamin." She filled another cup with water and handed it to me to drink.

I cleared the mucus out of my throat, spat in my spit cup, and quickly swallowed the pill in a hurry before the mucus built up in my mouth. To my surprise, the pill slid down my throat with no effort. "Open your mouth and lift your tongue," the nurse directed me. The nurse examined the inside of my mouth making sure I swallowed the pill.

Usually, my mornings didn't consist of me taking the humongous prenatal vitamin. It was hard for me to swallow pills, taking vitamins wasn't part of my daily regime. Furthermore, I was already sick from the pregnancy, taking the huge prenatal vitamin only made me sicker.

Here I was, 18 years old, about to graduate, and not to mention, have my first child; and, the system treated me no better than slaves were treated at auction when they stood on the wooden block to be sold. I was able to hurry back to my corner to spit in the space I had been occupying. Though, I wouldn't exactly call it a private place. I was sick and humiliated.

2 LIFE CHANGING JOURNEY

The second night, I laid there shivering. The night was long and left me with nothing but time to think about how I became me. My troubling thoughts always led back to my mother's first husband, Lucifer. I remembered waking up in the middle of the night to him rubbing my coochie. At night, he'd come into my room that I shared with my sister, stand over my bed, and molest me. He'd trace the outside of my vagina. Usually, I'd only muster up enough courage to hardly move. Mostly, I'd act as if I was sleeping and carefully turn onto my other side. Usually, Lucifer got the hint I was awake, and he'd leave me alone. I'd lay there, too scared to move and too scared to speak. My feelings and fear were unexplainable.

Lucifer repeatedly molested me, until it escalated to rape. It happened on an ordinary day. I was eight years old and in the third grade. On my way home, I picked weeds that grew through the fences of the houses I passed. As I passed the houses on the street, I was sure to stay on the sidewalk. My mother would whip the black off me if she caught me in the street.

The block had lots of old houses on the street. At the other end of the block was our low-income, two-bedroom, redbrick townhouse. We had a bath and a half and a full-unfinished basement. There were four townhomes lining Hamlet and 8th Street. We lived on that corner, right across the street from the Huckleberry House - a refuge for homeless teenagers and runaways. Across from the Huckleberry House stood another apartment building with approximately four floors of apartments. On the other corner, across from that apartment building and across from my apartment, was a building, which housed four other apartments. The rest of the street continued with old houses, one after the other.

I strolled as if I didn't have a care in the world. Usually, when I got home from school, I changed my clothes, had a snack, did my homework, later, Lucifer would drop my sister and me off at his mother's house.

Usually, when I got home, Lucifer and my sister would be waiting for me. And, any other day, he'd stick to our schedule, so he could get to work on time. Lucifer had to be at work at six and he didn't like being late. This day was different because he was relaxed, and my baby sister wasn't home.

When I stepped into the house, Lucifer was sitting

on the love seat. He motioned for me to sit beside him. I sat my book bag down, walked over, and sat down next to him. He put his arm around me, which made my body tremble and my breathing heavy. Lucifer was never nice to me. I could tell he didn't like me.

"How was your day?" Lucifer asked.

"Okay."

"Your mother wants you to clean your room. When you're done, let me know."

When I finished cleaning my room, I did as Lucifer told me. I went downstairs to let him know I was done. Lucifer was sitting there with a sneaky grin on his face.

"Come here girl," Lucifer demanded, in a somewhat playful manner. He sat me on his lap and from behind a pillow; he pulled out a pornographic magazine. I was frightened.

"Is your coochie as pretty as hers?" he asked pointing to a nude woman in the picture.

I didn't know what to say. I began trembling. I didn't know what he wanted to hear. Nobody ever asked me a question like that before. And I'd certainly, never thought about looking down there. In the picture, a white woman sat on a chair with her legs cocked open. She used her arms to hold her legs open and her hands to spread her vagina. The picture wasn't pretty or tasteful.

I looked at him and shamefully answered, "Yes."

I figured that if I gave him the answer he wanted, he'd leave me alone. As soon as those words left my tongue, my heart started to pound. I was sure; he could hear my heart pounding. My intuition warned me of the bad scene that was playing out.

"Let me be the judge." He grabbed me and threw me to the floor.

I screamed and struggled to get away, but he was too strong. I screamed with all my might, hoping the neighbors might hear me. It was hopeless. I tried to scream as loud as I could. Nothing was coming out of my mouth. Fear paralyzed my vocal cords; my voice was gone.

As I kicked, Lucifer held both my wrists down with his left hand. He sat on top of my left leg, preventing me from wiggling around. His right hand unbuttoned his pants. He unzipped my shorts and pulled them down along with my underwear. He pulled his penis out, held it, fondled it, moved it up and down, and massaged it. Once his penis was erect, he tried to force it inside of me. My vagina didn't let his penis inside.

His penis couldn't break through my vagina, but that didn't stop him. He took his penis, swung it back and forth, hitting my vagina, again, and tried to jam it inside me. I fought to free myself. I screamed as loud as I could. Again, I screamed. I only managed to get a little screech out. My voice went silent. I was physically screaming with my mouth wide open, but no sound was coming out. I was a screaming mute.

When Lucifer finished, he instructed me to wash up. I could barely walk. I took short, small steps, finally making it to the bathroom, which was a couple of feet away. I was in grave pain. I cried quietly. I went into the bathroom, closed the door behind me, and ran the cold water hoping to soothe my vagina. I was too scared to touch myself. I took the cool washcloth and patted my vagina gently. When I came out of the bathroom, Lucifer instructed me to get myself together. He acted as if nothing happened.

"Quit crying girl! You act as if you've just lost your best friend," he scolded as we walked to the car.

The truth was, I lost a piece of myself that day and a part of me died. He was never a friend to lose. We rode in silence to his mother's house. I dared not to look at him. He habitually smoked weed in his car and every time I rode in it, I fell asleep. But, not on this day, I kept my eyes wide open.

When we got to his mother's house, I didn't say anything to anyone that evening. My mother didn't believe me the first time I told – and as a consequence, I was afraid no one else would believe me. I tried to act normal for the remainder of the evening. Lucifer's young cousins asked me to play double-dutch. I loved jumping rope and was good at it, but I only offered to turn the rope. There was no way I could get my feet off the ground; I could barely walk. I had pain and pressure in my vaginal area.

When my mom got off work that evening, I remained silent. I didn't say anything all night. I didn't know who to trust. Previously, when I told my mom that Lucifer was molesting me, he made up a story and convinced her that I was dreaming. She believed him. I couldn't trust her to protect me. I didn't know what to do. I knew I didn't want him to rape me again.

The next day, I went to school and thought of the program that came to my school annually to speak with the students. The people in charge of the program stood in the front of the classroom and told us that we could trust them and tell them anything. They'd check the white kids for lice and announce if anyone in the class had something, they wanted to talk about to raise their hands. They had private conversations in the hallway. I had something to tell them and hoped they would come to the school that day. I waited all day, hoping the teacher would make a special announcement to the class about surprise visitors, but they never came.

I spent the entire day looking at the clock until the 3 o'clock bell rang. It rang louder than usual. I left school and I ran and ran and ran some more. I headed towards my grandparent's house. They lived three miles away. My school was located off Fourth Street, a busy street. I was afraid Lucifer would find me on the main roads, I ducked and dodged, running through alleys and downside streets, all the while looking behind myself the entire time. I didn't know what would happen if Lucifer caught me.

As I ran, my dry throat cracked as I breathed in and out. I was thirsty and needed a drink of water but kept running. I ran as fast as I could. I passed Chittenden Avenue and continued down Fourth Street heading north. When I came to a street that had access to an alley, I ran all the way down the alley as far as I could. My heart raced quickly.

Where the alley oddly ended, some apartments forced me to re-navigate my route. Two white kids playing in the street picked up rocks and threw them at me. I cried, but I continued running. I turned around and returned to Fourth Street, to get to the next street with access to an alley. I ran to the end of that alley, crossed the railroad tracks, and found myself at a warehouse store.

A police officer sat in his car in the parking lot of the store. I questioned if I should tell the police what happened. Then I convinced myself that I was close to my grandfather's house and I was confident that I could trust him. So, I kept running. I crossed the busy street and ran across the overpass of the highway and back to the first street that had alley access.

I felt safe being in a familiar neighborhood. I ran all the way down the alley for eight blocks, I got so comfortable, I stopped looking behind myself. When I turned the corner to my grandparent's street, I ran faster than I had ever run. When I reached my grandparent's house, I walked through the doors relieved, but exhausted. I walked into the house and my grandfather came from the kitchen surprised to see me.

"Where's your mother?" he asked.

I couldn't talk. I wanted to run into my grandpa's arms and wail my eyes out.

"Where is your mother?" This time he asked with a firm tone and bass in his voice. My grandfather was a tender man. When I did bad things, he never raised his voice at me. With my eyes wide open I tried not to cry, I looked at my grandfather, my grandmother, was now standing next to him. I took a deep breath, swallowed the swollen knot in my throat, and looked away.

My grandfather kneeled and looked me in the eyes in the most serious, but gentle way, and asked, "How did you get here, Keturah?"

In a quivering whisper, I managed to say, "I walked."

My grandfather asked again, "Where is your mother?"

"I don't know," I started to cry and couldn't stop.

"What's wrong? What happened?" I told my grandparents what Lucifer did to me the previous evening. My grandfather got on the phone and called my Aunt Harriet who was studying to be a lawyer. She told him, she'd come and take me to the hospital.

3 THE HOSPITAL

My Aunt Harriet and I walked through Children's Hospital emergency room doors. We looked around and found empty seats by the window. A television hung from the ceiling; and, in the furthest corner, a bunch of books sat on a large bookcase fixed to the wall. Left of the television and in the middle of the room colorful fish swam in a huge tank.

My aunt escorted me to a seat, and I sat down. She went to speak to a nurse, came back, and explained I had to go to a room alone with the doctors. She also explained that I would have my private parts examined. I paid close attention to what she was saying. I knew I was in good hands. I shook my head up-and-down, letting her know I understood. I didn't know what to expect in the other room, but I felt safe. The only person I feared at that point was my mother.

The nurse came over, took my hand, led me to an examining room, and closed the door behind us. The room was a typical hospital room, with a hospital bed, chair, and a stool placed underneath the desk.

The nurse pulled the chair close to the desk, and said, "Have a seat." She pulled out the stool and sat down next to me. The nurse asked me a series of questions and asked me to tell her everything that happened. Next, she handed me a diagram of a girl and a green marker and she told me to write an x on the body parts Lucifer touched.

I grabbed a pen and marked all the areas on my body that Lucifer violated.

"Did you take a bath this morning?"

"I took a bath last night," I corrected her.

Once I circled all my body parts on the diagram, the nurse gently said, "I'm going to step outside the room to let the doctor know you're ready."

I changed into the hospital gown and the nurse went to fetch the doctor. When she returned with the doctor, the nurse directed me to lay back on the bed and put my feet in the chrome stirrups. I was embarrassed and uncomfortable. I did as I was told and wished for them to hurry up. The doctor warned me, I might feel some discomfort.

He held up a long, thin stick that had a cotton ball on one end (looked like an extra-long Q-tip to me). Next, the doctor said he was putting the Q-tip inside of me to collect evidence. I looked up at him and nodded my head. The nurse stood by my side as I squeezed her hand. I didn't know that I had a hole down there before Lucifer tried to jam his penis in it.

After the doctor completed the examination, I joined my Aunt Harriet and the police officers waiting outside the examining room. My aunt grabbed my hand and looked at me and told me granddad had telephoned the hospital and told her that Lucifer was furious and was looking for us. He said he would kill us, and I was afraid he would do exactly that. The sun had already set outside of Children's' Hospital. The park located in front of the hospital had lots of large scary-looking trees creating large swaying shadows. It was a little before 10:00 p.m. as my aunt and I was quickly escorted to our car by two police officers.

My aunt drove behind our police escort as they led us to a brick building. The sign above the door had big blue letters that read Children's Services. After we were safely in the building, the police pulled off. We walked in the lobby of the office and a white woman greeted us. Because it was late, she was alone, as the other employees had probably left for the evening. The case worker introduced herself as Mona Kingsten and led us to her office.

"Do you mind talking to me in front of your aunt?" the woman asked.

I told her that I didn't mind and told my story, being sure not to leave out any details. After recalling the horrible event, Ms. Kingsten got a serious look on her face and asked, "Would you like to go home to your mother?"

I quickly replied, "No."

My mother always told me, "What happened in her house - Stayed in her house!" And I knew she'd scream and whip me for telling her business, as she had done many times before when she discovered that I had discussed her personal business with my grandfather.

Ms. Kingsten said we needed to call and talk to my mother. One of the most frightening moments of my life was when she dialed my mother's number. She spoke to my mother briefly. Then, she handed me the phone. I got nervous when I heard my mother's voice.

"Keturah, this is Mommy, why don't you want to come home?"

"Because I'm scared, you're going to whip me," I replied with tears streaming down my face.

"I'm not going to whip you, I want you to come home," she pleaded.

"I don't want to, I'm scared," I declared through streams of tears.

At that point, Ms. Kingsten took the phone and told my mother that my Aunt Harriet agreed to let me stay with her until the situation was resolved. I wanted to go home with my mother, but I was too frightened to risk getting screamed at or whipped. My intuition told me; it was in my best interest to stay with my aunt. Previously, when I told my mother that

Lucifer molested me, my mother broke her promise and let him come home. I, therefore, had a good reason not to trust her words or actions. At that moment, I grew up and started making my own decisions. I didn't know how important that decision was for me. That was a fundamental moment in my life.

After Lucifer was arrested for raping me, my aunt discovered he had an arrest record longer than the lines created when a new pair of Jordan sneakers come out on the market. His arrest record listed many disgusting sinful violations. He inflicted me with his sinful demons and because of him, my closet was full of sad memories. Thinking about Lucifer usually made me angry. I often wondered if I'd never met him, who I'd be.

When I thought of Lucifer, it automatically made me think of my mother's ultimate betrayal. I couldn't separate the two things. In all these years since Lucifer raped me, my mother has never explained why she stood by him, nor has she bothered to talk about the incident at all. I was angry with my mother because she never explained her position or apologized for failing to protect me when I needed her most.

My mother knew that I was aware that she testified in court on Lucifer's behalf. In an attempt, to protect Lucifer, she collaborated with him to create an alibi and reasonable doubt, testifying that I knew how to ride the city bus. She and Lucifer went as far as having some bus driver testify, he saw me riding the bus the day I ran to my grandparent's home. This was intended to convince the jury that I had not run all the way to my grandparent's house and was not truthful. My mother also testified that I was a very active child and had recently fallen off my bike and could have broken my hyman. That would explain my broken hyman and the remnants of blood found inside my vagina. The more I learned about her betrayal, the angrier I became. I'll never understand what Lucifer had over her.

I'll never understand why my mother allowed Lucifer to walk around the apartment naked. Through my cracked bedroom door, I saw the silhouette of his ding-a-ling flopping around. Sometimes, he came in my room nude and just stood over my bed with his piercing stare and deviant hands that ultimately intruded into my privacy and interrupted my restful sleep. I used to be a heavy sleeper before the molestation started. Afterward, I trained myself to sleep lightly.

My heart broke into many pieces knowing that my mother betrayed me by testifying that I knew how to ride a bus, and the other excuses she made to shade the truth. I was especially hurt because of the amount of courage it took for me to take the long, scary journey to my grandparent's house. Talk about insult to injury, my wounds were deep and salty. I couldn't understand for the life of me how she could love someone like him. "How could she love such a freak?"

Family is the First Teacher

Family is a universal concept. Most ethnic groups agree that the institution of the family is sacred. A social unit referred to as the nuclear family includes a mom, dad, and children. Extended family expands upon the nuclear family including grandparents, aunts, uncles, and cousins. The nuclear family is the first to educate a child. However, in many ethnic groups, the extended family has just as much impact on a child's life. A child is socialized by their nuclear and extended family.

The family is the first to teach a child about love, self-worth, fill the child with self-esteem, define family for the child, and much more. A collective mindset of the concept of love, self-worth, self-esteem, family, or the lack thereof are created and handed down from generation to generation. Families also share core principles learned and passed down to children. These core principles include values, customs, and beliefs.

Many teach their child values, customs, and beliefs usually in the same manner as they were taught. The child learns these fundamental concepts and family norms solely owned by that family. Therefore, it's important for families to take responsibility for how a child is nurtured and raised. A child should be raised and nurtured with the belief that they are worthy and respected as a person.

At my grandparent's house, the front door was always open, we kept our shoes on, there was always a hot meal made from scratch on the stove, and, we ate all day long. Their kitchen always had the latest updated amenities and technology: a dishwasher and microwave; and, they also had the coolest selection of cable T.V. channels with special cartoon shows specifically created for the entertainment of children. None of my aunts or uncles prepared their meals or set-up and tended to their homes the exact way my grandparents did. Each of them tweaked their household customs to their own liking, and over time, we became eight different families.

My experience growing up living in three different households: my mother's, aunt's, and grandparents had given me the opportunity to see the individual cultures and lifestyles that stemmed from the collective culture of my family. With-in our extended family, each household was different and run differently by that family member. Navigating these worlds as a child was difficult. When I moved in with my aunt, the subtle differences between her household and my mother's household were clearly prominent.

My aunt lived in a house that she was purchasing, when I went to live with her, I immediately recognized it was different in contrast to living in an apartment. I immediately noticed that the culture and rules were different from living in an apartment. My mother lived in an apartment that she rented. As renters and being on welfare, living in a low-income area, the neighborhood exposed us to cultural differences through the diversity of our neighbors. We encountered different cultures, income levels lower than ours, and vastly different lifestyles, all which created noticeable anxiety in my mother. For this reason, living in a house felt different to me, as it was more liberating. There was more privacy and space; and, I was able to play in the fenced-in backyard, which made me feel safer.

When we visited my Aunt Harriet's house and my Grandparents' house, my mother would allow me the freedom to play in the yard. This was contrary to the restricted apartment living, where my mother did not allow me to go off the porch. That is why I associated living in a house as a more liberating experience than apartment living. Though, it didn't matter whether I lived in a house or an apartment because my home was wherever my mother was.

Although my Aunt Harriet and mother have the same two parents and grew up in the same household, I quickly realized that they were different and lived different lifestyles. My mother was a strict disciplinarian and her home was full of rules. She was, what I called an over-protective, controlling, authoritarian. Furthermore, compared to my aunt's house, my mother's home was structured.

After school, my mother made me change out of my school clothes, gave me a snack, and like clockwork, I completed my homework. I had a strict bedtime at my mother's house too. My mother's house also included home-cooked breakfast, lunch, and dinner. We didn't have cable television, a dishwasher, or a microwave; and, my mother only allowed me to eat at the kitchen table. I shared a room with my sister at my mom's house, but I didn't mind that arrangement. Living with my mother was routine and ritualistic. Life was normally good before Lucifer moved in.

On the contrary, living with my aunt was quite different. My aunt was a busy career driven professional lady. She loved to shop and eat out at restaurants. It was obvious she had more money than my mother. When we went grocery shopping, my cousin and I each picked out our own box of cereal and our own snacks. Sometimes, my aunt would go through the trouble of taking us to the fast-food restaurant of our choice – which meant waiting in two or three fast-food driveways.

At my mother's home, I ate whatever she cooked. I had no choice in the matter, and she forced me to sit at the table until my plate was clean, no matter how long it took me. My aunt had cable T.V., enough money to buy me name brand sneakers, and, she was able to send me to St. Augustine Catholic School with my cousin. If we went somewhere after school, my aunt would look at me and ask, "Are you wearing that?" pointing to my Catholic school uniform and I would respond "Yes." I was proud to wear that uniform and to let others know that I attended Catholic school; and, I truly thought the uniforms were cute.

Living with my aunt was turbulent at times. Working full-time, Army National Guard one weekend a month, studying for the bar examination, and raising two pre-teens couldn't have been easy. The rules for my cousin were a little different, as well. My aunt allowed him to challenge her and he rarely complied with any of her rules. I instantly recognized this as a different form of expression. Although my aunt didn't care for my cousin's lack of respect, this new language was a phenomenon I had to try out for myself.

Due to my fear of my mother, my gull would have never seen the light. I quickly learned that my aunt didn't allow me to challenge her either. I didn't like the rules; my thoughts were if my cousin could do it, I could too. I recognized that mothers have a soft spot for their children. It was easier for my aunt to set boundaries for me than with her own son.

For this reason, for over three years, I went back and forth living with my Aunt Harriet and my grandparents, when I didn't get along with the other. Adjusting to their household rules and ways of life on a permanent basis was difficult. Although I was a part of the family, they all spoke different languages and the two households were different. It was difficult learning the language of each household; as difficult, as learning to speak the French language. Life was different outside of my mother's household.

It is more than notable for someone to voluntarily become a surrogate parent to someone else's child, especially under traumatic circumstances. It takes strong individuals like my Aunt Harriet and my grandparents to emotionally and selflessly invest their energy into a broken child. It takes a village to raise a child; and, no role is more important than any other.

No matter what happened between my mother and me, I found her presence undeniable and irresistible. No matter how broken our bond or how chiseled the pieces, a weak material such as masking tape was strong enough to mend our bond. However, our circle of trust was a completely different story. Restoring trust in my mother was more difficult, regardless of me loving my mother with all my heart. The relationship between a mother and child is often misinterpreted and misunderstood when judged by outsiders. Outsiders have their own biases, delusions, and experiences, which filters through and can only be characterized and described as unqualified judgment.

My natural place was with my mother. Naturally, my mother drew me to her, and I believed I drew her to me. On a greater level, no one understands our parent-child destiny. Some believe the bond between parent and child is unbreakable because through the bond exists a linked purpose in life only the two can achieve by working together. The full range of exchanges that take place between a mother and child are endless and priceless.

One lesson I learned from being separated from my mother, is that I didn't like being separated from her. I decided when I become a mother, I'll ensure that I'm never separated from my child. I am the only one that can define my mother's love for me. Because my love for my mother is unconditional, I'm able to accept her for who she is. Only those who believe in unconditional love can conceptualize this notion.

The Living Fear

For an entire year, I pretended to be sleeping when my mother came to my grandparent's house. I pretended so well; I often fell asleep. However, she never gave up trying to reach out to me. She did what responsible parents do, although I repeatedly rejected her attempts, she never gave up.

By my 11th birthday, mother had won me over; and, I wanted to be with her. However, my first reaction to her taking me out to celebrate my birthday was great fear. I still feared that she was upset about me breaking her rule by disclosing what happened in her house. I also feared that she was upset that I told on Lucifer and because Lucifer was in prison after being sentenced to 25 years to life. I was fearful, nervous, and confused and weighed down with mixed emotions. It was difficult to process for a child that was hardly 11 years old.

My mother picked me up from my grandparent's house on my birthday. I was staying with them at that time, who knows what disagreement my aunt and I had. As I said, I was both excited and scared, at the same time, to hang out with my mother. My mother got a car and learned to drive, that's one reason I was excited about hanging out with her. I was proud that she was taking me shopping and doing well for herself.

Of course, our first outing was a bit awkward. We

both proceeded with caution. When we arrived at the mall, my mother asked what I wanted for my birthday. I told her that all I wanted was a baseball cap. We went to the hat rack, and I searched through the baseball caps with short little sayings on them.

"Is that all you want?" my mom asked.

I couldn't think of anything else that I wanted, so she allowed me to pick out three caps. For the life of me, I can't remember the words written on two of the baseball caps. However, I will never forget my dark blue baseball cap with gray bubble letters that read "Why Me?" It took some time and work, but eventually, my fear of my mother slowly began to dissipate.

After Lucifer raped me, my overall experience with fear was different. My counselor gave me a book to read; and, the girl in the book experienced the same responses that I was experiencing. My fear was great and powerful that it came over me and tortured me at surprising moments. As described by the girl in the book, the fear was great that I would literally find a corner to ball up in and hide when the fear was around. My counselor told me that it was a common response experienced by rape survivors.

The dark shadow of fear hung around me for years, popping up unexpectedly. I could never connect or put my finger on why these emotions came over me, and why in the oddest moments. Years later, I realized, I was experiencing post-traumatic stress disorder (PTSD). I still occasionally experience fear, but when I do, I look at it as a challenge. Sometimes, I use it to be fearless, like the time I walked all the way to my grandparent's house after Lucifer raped me.

Ironically, when I stabbed Boomquifa, fear played more of a role as my accomplice than as my guardian angel. My main goal was to protect myself. I learned early in life at the ripe young age of eight, that running from my problems only created more problems. I learned if I faced and handled my problems, they didn't become aggravated, nagging problems.

By the end of my sixth-grade year, my Aunt Harriet was engaged to be married. She made plans for my cousin and her to move to Alabama, where her fiancé lived. They married soon after. Prior to her leaving, midway through the year, my mother and sister had moved into the house with my aunt. When my aunt moved, my mother continued living in her house. I remained in Columbus to be with my mother and sister.

I wouldn't have wanted it any other way. I'd already lost several years of valuable time being away from my sister. I was happy my mother and aunt agreed and made the decision to keep me in my rightful place, with my mother and sister. It was a smooth transition. My mother and I had been working on mending our relationship for some time at that point. It was easy for me because that's where I wanted to be, with my mother and my sister. When I didn't live with my mother, she wasn't an absent parent and I was never absent from her magnetic force.

4 ONE WEEK LATER IN DH

Processing my situation exhausted me and I was tired of thinking. I wanted to cry. I was mad and furious with my neighbors and myself. How did things get so out of hand? Boomquifa's family tried to delay the trial until my 18th birthday, hoping to have me tried as an adult, but it didn't work – not in this world anyway. I was totally unaware of my blessings.

One whole year passed before the trial; and in between that time, I had gotten pregnant. I thought about my boyfriend Jacob, my unborn baby, and the mess in which I inadvertently, involved innocent people. I never wanted to hurt anybody, not even Boomquifa. But I stand by the idea that they got what they deserve – touché.

I couldn't remember a Saturday night that lasted, long as my first Saturday night locked up. I thought I'd go crazy before a year passed me by. I planned to call Jacob and my mother every day. I was impressed that Jacob waited at my mother's house for my calls and surprised by how supportive he'd been.

My mother was disappointed when she found out that I was pregnant. She occasionally made a common threat known to many young black girls in America; eviction was a condition that came along with pregnancy. I was petrified to tell my mother I was pregnant. I had already confided to Phil, and he gave me time to tell my mother myself. One day after school, I made up my mind to confess.

Although I was home alone, my respect and fear for my mother were so great that I left the house. I went two doors down to my friend Ida's house. When we got to her bedroom and she sat down on her bed, her stomach poked out exposing her pregnancy. I slumped on her bed next to her.

"Girl, what's wrong with you?" Ida asked.

I covered my face before speaking. "I think I'm pregnant."

"Stop lying Keturah! You playin?"

When I looked her in her eyes, she knew I wasn't joking. I grabbed her hand and placed it on the lower part of my belly.

"Oh, Keturah! It is hard!"

"Do you think I'm pregnant?"

"Keturah," Ida whispered, "Keturah, it feels like you are."

"I don't want to join your gang," I said

respectfully, shaking my head from left to right. "I got to call and tell my mom, but I'm scared."

"You'll be fine! Look at me. I'm good. You'll be fine. Call her."

I picked the phone up and dialed my mother's work number. When she answered the phone, I didn't waste any time revealing my secret. My mom calmly told me we'd talk about it later that night when she got off work.

My mother and I talked that night and to my surprise, I didn't get the hellraising response I expected. My mother told me the choice was mine to make. But she kept it real too.

"You got yourself knocked up, now you don't have a choice but to be a mother. He has a choice. You have more to lose. You need to think about having this baby. Jacob's a playboy; he's not going to marry you. If you're betting on that, you'll lose."

My mother was incongruously supportive, but she was sympathetic to my situation. I understood that she didn't want me to play the fool.

#

I tried to process my shocking dilemma and the culture shock that came with it. Most of the other girls in Detention Hall were in for petty crimes like stealing and running away; they were there for a week to three weeks. I was yet to meet someone who'd gotten more time than I got and had no idea where my destination would lead me.

I was assigned to C pod, a unit for the older girls, fourteen and up. As one of the oldest girls in the pod, I felt out of place for many reasons; my age and pregnancy being the most obvious. It was quiet- time and all the girls were sitting at one of the two tables. The girls in my pod were fourteen, fifteen, and there was one other girl that was sixteen years old. The sixteen-year-old girl was Lucifer's cousin. Although I didn't know her well, her familiar face was comforting.

I sat at the table with a book in my hands. I was lost in my thoughts. I struggled to read the words on the page, the words collided with my loud thoughts. I didn't get through a single paragraph that morning. My thoughts and emotions ran as rapidly as my eyes ran over the words of the page. I thought about my upcoming graduation ceremony I was supposed to attend. I was devastated that I wouldn't walk the stage. On top of that, it was my first couple of days in juvie and I couldn't have any visitors. Visitors' day

Grandpa's Pound Cake

had already passed.

"How much time did you get?" Brownie inquired.

"I got a year," I answered.

"For what?"

"Felonious assault one."

Brownie sighed while shaking her head from side to side. "You're probably going to Scioto," she said confidently.

"No, my lawyer said I'm going somewhere I can keep my baby," I said with an attitude, hoping I knew what I was talking about. I only knew what I heard in court and the Magistrate said I get to keep my baby when it's born. I'd never heard of a facility called Scioto.

"But you can't keep your baby there. Are you sure? Most people go to Scioto if they have six months or more," Brownie added, sounding sincere.

"Well, all I know is what I was told," I snapped.

I clenched my fist. I lowered my head and got an instant headache. I didn't know what was going on, but I needed some answers. During visitation, I was going to demand that my mother be upfront with me. I told Brownie I didn't feel like talking anymore and went to sit alone at another table. I wasn't in control of my emotions. For the last two days, the moment I was alone, I cried like a baby.

I wished I would die. I was sick of spitting, being pregnant, and homesick, all at the same time. I wanted to run but couldn't. Break out of jail, but unable. I wanted to scream at the top of my lungs but couldn't. Physically and emotionally, I was confined. I couldn't cope with my situation. I didn't know how long I'd survive the misery and injustice in my life. I sat there silently screaming.

Tuesday rolled around and I'd survived a week not seeing my mother and Phil. While in the shower, I hacked until my mouth and throat were clear of the mucus that never seemed to go away. I spat all day, every day. I used the hot mist of the shower to clear my throat and to cover up the sound of my hacking and spitting, hoping I didn't gross out anyone. I dried myself off and applied lotion to my belly. I rubbed the lotion into my skin and sized up my stomach with my hands. It was amazing how much my stomach had grown in the last week. Four months pregnant and for the first time, I felt tiny flutters glide across the left side of my belly.

I put on my orange jumpsuit issued by DH. I was petite and no one could tell I was pregnant. I parted my hair down the middle of my head and sported two cornrows to the back, like Snoop Dogg. DH had a community curling iron, but I didn't feel like trying to get cute. I wasn't going anywhere. We had free time while waiting for the hour of visitation to begin.

"Andrew and Black," the guard called out. "The two of you line up."

I tried not to smile. The kids at school used to call me Blackie because of my last name. I was happy to hear my name, and happier to see my mother and Phil. I walked into the visitation room and spotted my parents right away.

My parents sat at a table in the middle of the room. I walked up and wanted to grab my mother and tightly squeeze her but kept my thoughts to myself. Phil got up and hugged me before I sat down. My mother looked at me, and I looked at her. My intuition told me she wanted to hug me, as much as I wanted to hug her. But, in all these years, she still hadn't learned to express the type of love I craved.

When my baby sister died of cancer a couple of years earlier, my mom didn't offer a hug or any display of affection, only small words that offered no comfort. I looked at my mother and could tell she'd been worrying. Right away, I tried to hide how scared I was. I didn't want to upset my mother.

The hour shrunk into seconds. Our conversation left me just as confused as before, but hopeful. My mother promised they were working on my early release petition. She said she understood how devastated I was. She also said she'd make it possible for me to talk to Jacob as much as possible. If she had to, she'd keep my baby when he/she was born.

The conversation sent fearful thoughts through my mind. I feared I'd lose my child to the system. I'd rather have an abortion than have someone else raise my child. In the past, my cousins were wards of the state, and I know for sure, some foster parents abuse their foster children. I returned to my cell still unsure of where I'd be locked up for the next year. I was confused as to whether I'd get to keep my child with me for the duration of my incarceration.

That night I slept lightly. I could hear the faint sounds of cars speeding up and down the highway. The chill of the night woke me up. I hated being cold. I rolled into a fetal position, put my head under the tiny, short, grayish-black wool blanket and adjusted it, then, cuffed the edges around my body creating an airtight cocoon. I tossed and turned, struggling to keep my cocoon airtight.

My thoughts were negative, dark, and exploding from wherever they were confined; orchestrated by the skeletons living in the darkest places of my memory. My skeletons were hard to bury. The negative seeds they planted, popped up in my head giving them life. I grew up petrified of scary characters from scary movies of the 90s. The only way I was able to sleep after watching them was by turning on my bedroom light and mimicking the mind over matter attitude that many of the movies forced you to have. To stay in control of my wandering thoughts, it was important to possess a strong mind and remain in control of my feelings. My training from my past and from watching scary films from the 90s was a great example of the strong mentality I needed to survive in DH. I had to control my mind, and nothing else mattered, but of course, the struggle was real.

I turned onto my right side, cuffed the blanket around my body, and tried to get comfortable. With my head under my cocoon, I lifted my head to spit in my cup, which I kept attached to my side. The mat was harder than a rock. I got out of bed, wrapped the blanket around my shoulders, walked the four corners of the cell, and then I stopped to look out the small window. The detention hall was located off Highway 70. From the cell window, I could see the big clock on the building adjacent to the building that held me. The view of Columbus downtown was great given the circumstances.

The Magistrate had stated that she sentenced me to 1-2 years in confinement because of my past with Lucifer. She suspected rage led me to take my past out on the monsters next door. I thought about the tragedies I'd been through in the last 11 years; more tears hijacked down my cheeks. I thought to myself, God knows that I have been through enough. I was scared and worried about raising my child and being a single mother in jail.

I couldn't get the words of the Magistrate out of my head. What did she mean by saying I was like a time bomb, holding in pain I'd endured over the years because of the rapist and the death of my sister? She said she was shocked I hadn't exploded years ago. I agreed with the Magistrate to a degree, the pressures of life often boiled over into my temper.

However, I didn't deserve being locked up for 1 to 2 years. It wasn't fair that I was being solely held responsible for the entire ordeal when what happened was not all my fault. If the Magistrate had any compassion at all, she would've sentenced me directly to a treatment center, instead of re-victimizing and traumatizing me.

#

The next morning during snack time, Brownie and I sat at a table talking. A guard brought our snack in, and to my surprise, it was a slice of pound cake. The pound cake looked like the one that my grandfather baked, it had white smooth looking icing melted over its top. However, DH pound cake didn't smell or taste like my grandfather's pound cake.

"This pound cake is hard and dry," I told Brownie.

She said, "Yeah, - we can probably pound cake ourselves out of here!" We both laughed.

"My grandfather makes the best pound cake. You haven't tasted any until you've tasted his. He makes it for me all the time. The most important ingredient he adds is a pound of love," I said while nibbling on the hard pound cake.

"I never knew my grandparents. Mine all died before I was born."

"That's sad. I've always been close to my mom's

parents. I've never spent much time with my paternal grandparents or with my biological father, but I've always had my mother's parents around."

Later, that day, one of the teachers at DH informed me that my teachers from my high schools, Brookhaven and Fort Hayes Career Center, were urgently trying to deliver my finals to me, and he expected them to arrive in the next day or so.

That evening, a guard delivered our mail when we were halfway through our free time. The guard handed me a letter. I told Brownie I'd be back after reading the letter from my mother. It appears that throughout the school and up and down my street "The L Block" as we called it, word spread about the Magistrate locking me up. My mom said quite a few people had asked about me.

The Forces of Four Walls

I had so much on my mind that I hadn't prepared myself mentally to move to Scioto Valley for Girls. Brownie was right after all. Earlier that day, they released Brownie, I was happy she wasn't around to rub in the fact that she was right. I sat on the temporary bed, rubbed my eyes, and prayed I'd survive my current tragedy so I could give my child a good life. I laid on what I called a mat of concrete until I fell asleep. I woke up with my stomach feeling heavier than usual.

I looked down at my stomach and was sure it had grown overnight. I got my meds and a guard told me I'd leave for Scioto after breakfast. The guard tightly fastened handcuffs and shackles to my hand and feet before we left the detention hall. The handcuffs and shackles totally caught me off guard. I never expected to be treated like a real criminal. Reality checked me. I was no different from any of the other girls locked-up.

I had to stay strong to get my seed and me the hell out of that situation. I was born fighting and learned over time I had to take care of myself. After Lucifer raped me, I promised myself, I would never ever let anyone hurt me again. I didn't start fights, but I was sure to finish them. I learned to speak up and take risks. Consequences for remaining silent were far worse than getting beat down or raped. I let my enemies know, a feud with me was a never-ending battle, and for sure, the fight wasn't over until I said so.

My friends always said I had little people's syndrome. I was tough for a short, petite girl. All the kids on my block knew I got down for mine if I had to. I'd gotten in fights every year since the fourth grade. In a way, everybody I'd fought before stabbing Boomquifa was partially responsible for my mindset at the time of the stabbing, right? Maybe I smelled like a sweet target because people always wanted to test me, especially big fat girls.

My courage deserted me the day the Magistrate locked me up. On one hand, I didn't have the energy to be tough, and on the other, I didn't want to get into any trouble. I kept my mouth shut so I could get out - anticipating an early release. I chose to play the innocent, good girl role. The girl that didn't smoke weed or drink. If I weren't pregnant, I would've played a virgin too.

When I arrived at Scioto, my stomach tied itself in knots. The jail life wasn't for me. Two entire weeks passed since I'd seen home. This was far from a vacation away from my parents. The guard led me through two large glass doors. The lobby was fancy; it reminded me of an expensive, modern hotel lobby. To my surprise, it looked nice and clean.

"Not again!" I thought to myself as a guard interrupted my observation of the lobby with the humiliating security process; telling me to pull my pants down, bend over, and cough. The guards could see my butt cheeks and my vagina hole. That place was a trigger for bad memories; talk about being institutionalized and traumatized repeatedly. The guards forcing me to show my vagina didn't feel right.

I followed the guard who led me to my assigned cottage. On the property of Scioto, which mirrored the design of a university campus, there were three cottages housing the inmates, a nurse's station, an auditorium, and a cafeteria. The guard walked me to the cottage called "Allman." They assigned me to the cottage that held the aggressive and older population of girls.

The cottage was shaped like a pentagon. There were cells on all five sides of the cottage, empty community space in the center of the cottage, a meeting room in one of the corners, a closed office for the guards, and a guard's station placed near the entrance.

The guard put me in a cell with two bunks and closed the door behind me. There was nothing else in the cell to describe, except for the four white walls, a bunk bed, and a young, blond, skinny white girl.

5 UNLOCKING PRIVACY

The next morning, I woke up in a different world. Scioto differed from DH; I saw the differences as two negatives. There were two community toilets and I had to share a cell which meant less privacy than before.

I woke up with a headache, my stomach ached, and I had horrible heartburn. I knocked on the door but couldn't hold it in anymore. I puked right in my spit cup. Puking on top of my spit was nasty, but they didn't authorize me to have a trashcan in my cell. I had to negotiate to keep my cup, I did what I had to do.

When I got sick like that, I had to wait for the first available opportunity to wash my cup. This meant, spitting on top of puke. If the cup overflowed, I dumped the puke in a sock, which acted as a sponge absorbing my liquid spit, capturing the thick mucus and toilet paper that I stuffed into my cup to absorb the fluids. All I had to do was meticulously turn the sock inside out, wash it, and hang the sock to dry. I was able to clean up my mess quickly, which was a great jailhouse invention.

All the girls pulled a chair to the lines that formed a square and outlined the community space. We sat in the square silently waiting for roll call and our morning meeting to start. The meetings usually consisted of us taking attendance, talking about the business of the day, and addressing any issues or gripes amongst the girls.

"Bitch you shut up; you were licking my pussy last night!" Ashley yelled. She and the other girl, obviously lovers.

Everyone stopped and focused on them, shocked they got away with getting out of their rooms, only to air their nasty, trashy business. As a result, they were punished for airing their business. Most of the girls snickered and started side conversations of their own. I mostly found it amusing.

I couldn't believe my ears. How were they able to get to one another, I wondered because we had to knock to get out of our cells? The gay activity was weird too. I wasn't used to seeing gay activity. Where I came from, our culture frowned upon it. Although the rules prohibited sexual activity at Scioto, it didn't stop stories from spreading about who was hooking up with who. For the duration of their stay, many of the girls became assimilated actors in their unnaturally controlled environment, submitting to an alternative state to have their sexual needs met.

The sexual tension was so bad, the guards made rules, prohibiting fruit that resembled a penis from leaving the cafeteria. Prison is the worst experiment known to humankind. The effect of locking up children at the height of puberty, and only exposing them to the same sex, has reared its full effects on our society. I hold the system responsible for plaguing the black community with the spirits of homosexuality because of the pipeline to prison. The plague is like cancer, it's strong, mobile, and mutates.

Locking children up in unnatural environments changes the way their brains form. Puberty is a crucial time when the brain is adjusting and regulating reality. Holding children in prison for long periods of time in unnatural states may cause the impressionable to believe that certain behaviors are their natural state. That is what they have come to know and like – their new normal. Many children begin to believe unnatural behavior is normal behavior. Though, whether they come to know or believe this behavior is unnatural or not doesn't matter, because it's what they ultimately begin to like and accept, it's their reality.

Some girls had sexual experiences with other girls, other girls used fruit to masturbate, and other girls were rumored to be under investigation for sleeping with the guards. This place wasn't suitable to rehabilitate or provide mental health treatment to children. The pipeline to prison was flooded with young girls like me; being held in inappropriate places, far from being in their best interest. Subject to a form of slavery built to break the spirit of any human being.

"Settle down!" The guards yelled. Ashley and Kennedy were placed on restriction for the next couple of days. Everyone knew Kennedy was a true bull dagger, inside and outside the jail walls. She dressed and acted like a boy; and, looked like a boy too. Today's society refers to people like her as transgender. I was in disbelief that a girl would lick another girl's coochie. The cultural shock made me squirm in my seat. But like the rest of the bunch, that didn't stop me from being nosy. Most importantly, I wanted to know how they got out of their cells.

#

I didn't make any friends at Scioto. I stayed to myself. I was one of the few loners. I didn't want any trouble. I only wanted to do my time and go home. I had a couple of conversations with other loners but didn't befriend anyone.

For daily conversation, I relied on my roommates. I had three roommates while at Scioto. My first roommate, Peyton, the young, skinny, white girl – the smart aleck, nobody liked; well, I was happy to get rid of her. She talked too much, and she got on my nerves. Ever since I was a child, I was like a magnet, drawn to people no one else liked. I always believed those people were misunderstood and if people took the time to notice their pain, they could be reached. I believed that I was born with this intuitive skill and was in tune and conscious when I share space with others. I feel and can almost translate their energy into feelings.

Peyton was a young troublemaker. She'd been through hardships; I'd gathered that she brought some of it on herself. Besides the abuse her father put her through, the fourteen-year-old talked about prostituting as if it was fun. She had a bad attitude too; but sometimes, I thought she was funny because the girl had the balls of a big girl. She didn't mind getting her ass kicked. She'd argue with anyone looking for a fight which drew negativity her way. Occasionally, I'd hear her arguing with someone about something stupid.

Olivia, my third roommate, was a nice black girl; but she had problems too. I assumed some of her problems were mental. Her mentality was different from anyone I'd ever met. She reminded me of an older woman with her own way of thinking. She was a prostitute too, but a different breed from my previous roommate. Olivia was about her money. The only reason I didn't like rooming with Olivia was that she literally rocked herself to sleep. She sucked her thumb and rocked back and forth all night long until she fell asleep.

Before leaving Scioto, I'd heard Olivia was under investigation for sleeping with a guard. She never mentioned anything to me, but the grapevine talks. Olivia wasn't the only girl under investigation though; there were a couple of other girls on the list. I recently searched Olivia's name on the internet and discovered she died three years after the time we spent together in Scioto.

I wondered how many girls were sexually abused by a guard. I often wondered if any of those girls were victims of human trafficking. I hadn't seriously considered the possibilities before. It would take years for social service professionals, lawmakers and politicians to agree some forms of prostitution are not a victimless crime. Later, treatment models would change from prosecuting the prostitute to a victim-based treatment model, where help and services became available for victims.

In 1996, no one knew how much human trafficking would grow and largely affect girls at the average ages of twelve to fourteen. Some of the girl's home lives and lifestyles put them at a greater risk of becoming a victim; that and the crack epidemic left many children fending for themselves. Every time I heard one of the girl's life stories, I realized how dull mine was, and how lucky I was. I've always had someone in my life that I could count on; and, my cup has always been half-full because of my guardians. A generous omniscient force has always protected me. Some of these girls weren't that fortunate.

Some girls didn't have a grandfather, a mom, a Phil, an Aunt Harriet, a cheerleading coach, or anybody else to remind them that in life, it's never too late to shine brighter than any star. My guardian angels were a part of my village of supporters that supported me in some of the darkest moments of my life. Looking back at those moments, I see that my guardian angels were my light and lifeline. Some injuries, whether mental, emotional, physical, or spiritual take longer to heal and process; but under the guidance of guardian angels, these experiences can be less painful.

These girls had real problems, worse than mine. "Who said life is fair," is one of the most powerful phrases I've heard. Life was full of twists and hard knocks for every girl that shared her story with me. A powerful association links us all together and to Scioto Valley for Girls. We will never be able to answer the question of why our paths crossed at that time and in that place.

#

I received a letter from my mother, which read:

June 3, 1996

"How are you holding up? Keturah, I know it's hard for you to be there, but be strong and hold your head up. You did nothing wrong to be there and no matter what; I will always be there for you until the end.

Keturah, I'm okay, it's just hard for me to see you there when we know the truth. I read your poem and it was good, but your thoughts at that time were about what was happening to you. Keturah, we have shared some things in both of our young lives, good and bad. You are my firstborn, and I have always loved you. I know you love me, and that makes us a whole as one.

Keturah, we're going to pull through this together. We are both strong women and I know we can make it. When they took you from that courtroom, it was as if they took a part of me away too. Why? I asked myself - but I got no answer. All I know is, when you try to do right, people try to hold you back if they can. But, they can't, if we don't allow or want them to - but not if I have anything to do with it. I always say, it is not over until the fat lady sings, and believe me; you will overcome all of this! Those fatsos next door can laugh and talk, but they're not happy; whatever someone does, comes back on them in a harder way!

Well, I sent you a box with hair gel, envelopes, conditioner, shampoo, hot oil grease, ponytail holders, nail files, a book of stamps, and another letter. Let me know if you receive them. Here's Jacob's number xxx-xxx-xxxx. He was here Sunday, but we didn't get a call from you. Well, let me know if you receive this letter and the items, I sent you."

Love always,
Your mother

Visitation at Scioto

After eating the heartburn spaghetti for lunch from the worst cafeteria in the world, it was time for visitation. The CO called all the girls who had visitors, which usually were the same girls. Some girls never got visitors. It's sad to think that some of the girls were there so long, their families and friends probably forgot about them. I pitied the foster children, and especially, the girls convicted for killing their mothers – some of them, didn't have anyone to visit them.

I walked through the cafeteria still lingering with the smells of the spaghetti we had for lunch. My mother and Phil sat at a table and I watched them staring me down as I walked toward the table. Phil stood up and gave me a warm hug and kissed me on my cheek. He transferred powerful energy, giving me a boost of love and positive energy. My mom sat there, looked up at me, and smiled. She didn't realize how much I needed her to wrap her arms around me.

"Your stomach's getting big," my mom broke the ice.

As I sat down. My mom pulled out a deck of playing cards from her purse. Throughout the visit, I mustered up the energy to laugh a few times. As we played cards, I discreetly pointed out the girls and whispered their reasons for being there. My mom and Phil were shocked at the severity of some of the crimes.

"Aye, I've heard some scary stories about some of the girls in my cottage. They said, one girl, killed her mother, dragged her down the stairs to the basement, and had a party. And, she's not the only one who killed her mother," I pointed to the girl on the side of us sitting with her grandparents.

"She looks too young to be in your cottage," Phil said.

"She is young, she's only twelve, and she's in here because she and her mother were fighting over a gun and her mother got shot. I heard her grandparents just started visiting her because the family was mad at her at first. I don't know the whole story, but what

I've heard so far is sad."

"Well, you mind your own business and stay on your best behavior because we're working on your early release. You have no priors; you were a good student with a job – you were defending yourself - I don't know why they were this hard on you. People believe this isn't fair, and we're going to do everything we can to get you out of this place," my mom said.

"Five minutes!" the guard announced loudly.

By the end of the hour-long visit, we'd played three hands of spades. I gathered the cards and handed them to my mother. Phil hugged me, and we said our good-byes. I walked into the small room, no bigger than a closet. If an inmate had any contact with the outside world, it was the procedure for the guards to search for us before they permitted us to go back to our cottage. The CO patted around my pregnant stomach, underneath my bra, instructed me to pull down my pants and underwear, bend over, and told me to cough. I never got used to that procedure.

I tried to keep my spirits up after each visit. I hated my parents leaving me in prison and rejoining the free world. Knowing I lived in a free world made it harder for me to accept my sentence. I knew jail was a place I could never come back to. Jail brought out the pain I didn't know existed.

I spent most of my nights laying wide-awake thinking of how I could change my situation. I wanted to reverse the hands of time and erase much of my life. I knew that at any moment things could turn from worse to horrible and from horrible to tragic. Over the years, I often felt dark remnants of my experiences following me around like a shadow. My experiences ascended and descended like a teeter-totter. My life was bipolar, a highway with extreme highs and lows, and, I always found myself bracing myself, waiting for the next big wreck to happen.

But, in my darkest moments, there was a glimmer of light. I was in jail for a little over a month, and although I was in a dark place, I did not forget what my mother told me. I stayed to myself, stayed on my best behavior, and bit my tongue anytime it wanted to flex. I was hopeful of an early release.

The thought of an early release and thoughts of my unborn baby were the main source of inspiration keeping my spirit and hope alive, because both represented a new beginning for me. My baby was a single thought and idea regenerating my spirit and keeping my recycled strength cycling. These two things gave me a reason to want to live. I didn't know how long they'd keep me motivated though.

Outside my cell, I could hear Ashley screaming at the top of her lungs. I laid in my bed and tried to think of good thoughts. My thoughts couldn't silence her screams. It sounded like they tied her down to that restraining table again. All I could hear was her big mouth. I was tired of her being on suicide watch. She made the environment stressful.

"I gotta pee!" Ashley screamed, "I said, I have to pee! - you fucking idiots!" That girl screamed for over an hour, cussing and talking shit. "Untie me from this table bitch!"

I put my hands over my ears, closed my eyes, and hummed. It was just as hard to block Ashley out, as it was to block out the irritating 24-hour nightlight. I missed my privacy and wanted out of there. I closed my eyes and tried to imagine something wonderful.

6 GRANDPA'S POUND CAKE

The next few weeks were routine for the most part. The rules permitted us to eat for 20 minutes and the guards ordered us not to talk. Everyone sat down and ate quickly. I ate as much as I could, as fast as I could. I couldn't keep up with the rest of the girls, smashing their food in their mouths, chewing a couple of times, and swallowing.

I wanted to finish my meal to the end, but it seemed impossible. Although I had regained most of my strength, my fragile ninety-eight-pound body, was struggling to gain back the 26 pounds I lost in the last 4 months. On top of that, I still couldn't swallow my own spit. The doctor said I was losing nutrients from spitting, and unhelpfully, hadn't suggested any remedies that worked.

I was surprised none of the guards or other girls said anything about how gross I was for spitting and hacking in the cup. As I sat there eating, I couldn't help but to suck the mucus out of my throat, spit it out, eat a spoonful of the scrambled eggs, and attempt to swallow quickly without making myself sick. My life was a disaster and I needed my mother.

As a child, I was quiet and shy. When my mother and I visited unfamiliar places, I'd cling to her. My mother would shake me off her leg like a puppy and shoo me away and tell me to go play with the rest of the kids. I think that sometimes quiet people, especially children, make other people nervous. People usually don't know how to treat their awkwardness. I guess for some, the quiet and shyness irk their nerves. Or, maybe they're offended that the quiet shy child didn't take to them.

Quiet children are often misunderstood as little human beings. There could be a plethora of reasons as to why quiet children feel uncomfortable, and equally, why they might make other people feel just as uncomfortable. But at the end of the day, everybody needs at least one person to pay attention to him or her and unconditionally love him or her. That's what my grandfather did for me; he loved me unconditionally. My happiest childhood memories are of me spending time with my grandfather.

My grandfather was slender, six feet tall, with a golden light brown complexion, and a comedic personality to go along with his great sense of humor. My grandfather was a skilled man. He was my hero, my Superman, my Popeye. My grandfather had muscles like Popeye, and we both ate spinach like Popeye too. Not only was my grandfather strong, but he was also an intelligent man. He knew everything about plumbing, gardening, and fixing cars; he could fix anything.

I spent every weekend at my grandparent's house. My grandfather would pick me up on Friday evening after work and drop me home on Monday morning. I never kept secrets from my grandfather and would blab all my mother's business to him, which was against my mother's rules. And, I paid dearly for my offense, with a whipping every Monday morning, before school. My mother continuously reminded me, "What happens in my house – Stays in my house!"

"What happens in my house - Stays in my house!" is an abusive, dangerous, problematic ideology and custom that should not be practiced! The practice puts children at risk for abuse. Enforcing that philosophy in households is at-risk parenting at best. Parents shouldn't do anything in front of children that cannot be repeated or shared. That is why I loved summer.

I didn't have to worry about my mother's business in the summertime. Every summer, I spent the entire summer with my grandparents. I'd help my grandfather till the earth, pull the weeds, and plant fruits and vegetables in a sectioned off part of his property. We planted cucumbers; tomatoes; red peppers; collard and mustard greens, and squash - my favorite vegetable. My grandfather cooked yummy good squash and eggs, fresh biscuits, and poured me a tall glass of orange juice for breakfast. Yum!

My grandfather was famous for baking pound cake. His pound cake was special. Not only did it taste good, his main ingredients included a pound of sugar, pound of butter, pound of flour, and, a special ingredient, a pound of love. His positive energy and love made his pound cake better than anybody's pound cake. And every time he baked pound cake, he baked enough to share with everyone. His pound cake was just one way he expressed and shared his unconditional love.

While gardening, my grandfather shared his life stories with me. He taught me lessons, some of which, I'd heard repeatedly. It was no secret that I was granddad's favorite grandchild. Our blood was tangled together, our lives paralleled, and, our experiences aligned, just at different times.

My grandfather was born in a log cabin in Stone Mountain, Virginia on September 1, 1926. Both of his parents came from families that owned farms. He lived on his maternal grandparent's farm from birth to the age of thirteen. He lived there with his mother, siblings, and maternal grandparents. He is the second child, the first son of five siblings.

My grandfather told me that he remembered the Great Depression and Jim Crow era, which progressed throughout his adolescent years. He said his family being poor didn't bother him; owning a farm was beneficial because they always had enough to eat. His family grew and hunted everything they ate, and his mother made all their clothing. He explained that he lived in the barter system days, where people traded goods and other resources for what they needed. Sugar and salt were the only goods his family didn't grow on the farm.

When he spoke about his childhood, I usually found myself absorbing his words as I pictured my Great-great-Grandfather and Grandfather walking side by side, wearing overall pants as the pair headed down a dirt road to trade a rabbit, or some wheat, for salt and sugar. The imagery wouldn't be as interesting if I didn't imagine my grandfather carrying his first rifle his grandfather had given him. My grandfather told me that everyone worked to eat in those days, kids too. When his grandfather went out to farm or hunt, so did he.

While working on the farm, side-by-side and, spending time with his grandfather, my grandfather said it was there, listening to his grandfather's stories, was where he learned work and love ethics. His grandfather taught him to work hard and love harder. My grandfather learned a love language equal to the greatest expression of love. He never had to tell me he loved me; I just knew from the way he treated me. He loved his family; we all meant the world to him. He was one person each of us could count on, no matter what type of trouble we got into; whether it was household plumbing issues, car trouble, jail, just about any trouble that came our way. Granddad ran to the rescue to bail out any of us. I can't think of one time when he let me down.

My grandfather displayed his tender and most sensitive side when he recited his oldest memory. When he was 3 years old, his 18-month-old sister died from whooping cough. When he told me this story, tears slid down his face. I didn't understand his pain until I lost my sister. Although my grandfather was only three when his sister died, he still vividly remembered when he and his older sister touched her small, cold, stiff body. They didn't realize their baby sister was dead until she didn't move. Six years stand between the death of his baby sister and the births of his two younger siblings.

My grandfather described his mother as a devout Christian woman. She forced him and his older sister to attend church a couple of times a week. There was no way of getting out of going because the church was located on their farm. The school building, however, was so far away his mother taught them the ABCs until he and his sister were able to walk to school on their own.

My grandfather and his older sister started formal school at the same time; he was seven and she was eight. The school they attended was one building with two classrooms. First, second, and third-grade classes were held in one classroom. The fourth and fifth graders were in the second classroom. Being an A student and the best speller in the class was one of my grandfather's best accomplishments in grade school.

One memory he recalls from his school days is the teacher swatting students that didn't complete their homework. He said he never got any swats. My grandfather laughed at his sister always wanting to carry the schoolbooks they shared, although, she was not as good a student as him. However, his sister had a more dominant personality than him. He recalled when they were younger, she knocked a boy down for repeatedly bullying him. Because his sister was more dominant and protected him, he learned he could count on his sister's superior dominance to take care of his conflicts. Ever since these early experiences, he avoided conflict at all costs and expressed that he did not allow such circumstances or situations to bother him.

Throughout his childhood, his father traveled back-and-forth to West Virginia to work as a coal miner, which resulted in the two of them spending little to no time together. Without his father around, he gravitated towards his grandfather, who was more like a father figure. His grandfather influenced and shaped him to be a model grandfather, which my grandfather paid forward to his grandchildren; the same love and care he received.

At thirteen, his mother took him and his sibling on a train and headed to Columbus, Ohio to live with her brother because she grew tired of his dad's infidelity with a woman in the area. The separation between his parents impacted his life greatly. This is when he realized he was poor. My grandfather says he got his first real job at age thirteen manually resetting pins at a bowling alley. During WWII, without his mother's consent, he changed his age from 15 to 18 and enlisted in the Navy. The limited job market in the area, ads asking for a few good men, and the hardships his family faced since they moved to Columbus persuaded him to do this. He explained that he went to the Navy because he was his own man.

Because my grandfather was the oldest son, he believed it was only fitting without his father or grandfather around that he stepped in to help his mother. However, his mother found out about him joining the Navy and went through a lengthy process to drag him home.

My grandfather and his sister attended high school until the twelfth grade and quit to work full-time jobs due to finances and other daily challenges. They both explained that they got tired of being poor and didn't want to attend school in the rags they described as oversized hand me downs from their cousins. They both laughed at the thought of my slender grandfather in their cousin's oversized overalls. My grandfather explained that, in those days, working was more important than school.

After the age of thirteen, my grandfather rarely saw his father. He explained that because his dad worked and traveled back-and-forth to West Virginia, he was used to his father's absence and was not greatly impacted by the greater distance between them when he relocated to Columbus. Consequently, moving further away made the distance between him and his father grow permanent. After the move and before the death of his father, he saw his dad a few more times. Although my grandfather did not express the impact moving away had on his life, his involved parenting style and stories told me differently. The stories of his life on the farm were utopia type stories about stability, positivity, and happiness, compared to the stories he shared about his life once he moved to Columbus. Life in the city was harder on the family socially and financially.

Later that evening, I didn't call Jacob. Instead, I called to speak to my grandfather. His rumbly voice greeting me on the other end of the phone offered me some comfort.

"Granddad, what-cha doing?"

"Oh, I ain't doing nothing, but going over my numbers and watching Wheel of Fortune."

"What's grandma doing?"

"She right here next to me," Granddad answered.

"How are you holding up? How you been feeling?"

I always became emotional the moment someone expressed genuine concern and compassion for me. Tears swelled up and I silently took a deep breath to manage my voice. I pulled the phone away from my mouth and spat in my cup, adjusted the receiver of the phone, and lied. "I'm fine."

My grandfather didn't make a fuss over my response. "You know, when I moved to Columbus it was different than rural Stone Mountain, Virginia. In Columbus, Jim Crow laws were enforced everywhere, he explained. Jim Crow laws bothered me none; that's just the way things were. I learned to respect authority and the social order. I bothered nobody, and nobody bothered me. I knew Jim Crow laws and the social order were unjust, but I didn't let it bother me."

I didn't know where he was going with this story. I just hummed, "Ummhm" in agreement.

"I married your grandmother at the age of twenty-six. Your grandmother was eight-teen years old, about your age now. We were married at a chapel located on Cleveland Avenue. Your grandmother's brother and wife stood as our witnesses. Keturah, keep this between you and me. Your grandma and I weren't married when your grandma had Uncle Cesar and not too many people know this."

My grandfather bonded me to secrecy. "I ain't gone say nothing," I promised.

You know in our day that's something we didn't make public. As you know, we had seven children, four girls, and three boys. But did you know 14 years stand between your Uncle Cesar and your Aunt Eve? For 14 years, your grandmother and I were having children.

"I didn't know that," I said. "That's a long time."

"Before I found stable employment, I worked hauling coal and on the railroad. At age thirty-six, I got a stable job with benefits at the State Hospital as a custodian and worked my way up to obtain a promotional position as a plumber. Although the State Hospital was a decent paying job, Grandma and I worked two jobs and struggled to care for our children. Because of our hard work, we managed to buy our first home in 1967.

We were the first black family on the street, besides a mixed couple living across the street. We were poor, but we managed to give our children a decent life. Although life has many scary, sad moments, focus on happy moments rather than the negative ones. I've learned growing old is somewhat scary; however, if you want to live, you cannot let fear, or any other obstacle stop you. Choose your battles wisely by only fighting things worth fighting. Now, it's your turn to give your child a decent life."

"I will granddaddy," I said.

After we said our goodbyes, my grandfather left me with our family's lineage and legacy to consider.

My family seemed to have unnecessary secrets. My grandparent's secret didn't change how I felt or what I thought about them. It didn't make any difference to me whether they were married or not before they had children. I don't understand how adults expect children to learn from experiences if the adults are too scared and untruthful about their own experiences and sins.

You can't tell your children to do as I say, and not as I do. That's like telling someone you've been somewhere but leaving out the important details and facts, as to how you got there, what you saw, what you experienced, and how you handled that experience. Because parents withhold information from their children, the natural reaction for a child is to go to the source to experience it for themselves.

Working through family sins and problems, and not fully understanding the true essence of the sins or problems creates a cycle to be continuously repeated. Many of my family members are repeating some of these same issues. Because no one knows the truth about my grandparents, we have and are still working through the vicious cycle of unwed pregnancies; none of my aunts or uncles in my family was married before having children. Now, I was about to add to the legacy of being an unmarried mother.

7 GRADUATION CEREMONY

I grabbed my cup, sucked all the mucus out of my throat, and hacked into the cup. DJ Kool's "Let Me Clear My Throat" often played in the back of my mind when I cleared my throat. I grabbed my housecoat and the panties Scioto gave me tagged with my name. Every item supplied by Scioto had my name on them: my housecoat, my socks, and my panties. On some of the items, they tagged my name on top of the names of those who wore the items before me.

I got in the shower and wailed. All I could think about was that I was missing my graduation day. If I were home, I would've walked the stage. Boomquifa and the system cheated me out of something I worked hard to accomplish.

I went to my cell and nudged Peyton to go take her shower. Peyton didn't have to knock on the window because I left the door cracked so she could get out. I needed a few more minutes alone to drown in my troubles. When Peyton returned from the shower, my eyes were red and puffy, and I was wailing uncontrollably.

Peyton went and told the guard. I overheard Ms. Villa's reply, "She shouldn't have done whatever she did, - I don't care about that girl crying. So, what, she missed her graduation, she had no business doing what she did to get in here!"

Peyton tried to comfort me with her sympathy, but I didn't say anything. I just kept crying. I was upset more by Ms. Villa's comments. Ms. Villa spoke loud enough for me to hear; I suppose that was her intention. That made me upset. I wanted her to care. Ms. Villa was heartless and lacked the slightest compassion, sympathy, and empathy. I determined quickly, I didn't like her, and she wouldn't be offering me a slice of pound cake.

I had a hard time dealing with not walking the stage. I was a good student, who often, made the honor roll. Everyone expected me to go to college after high school, which was my expectation too. I was no goody two shoes or anything. I never thought I'd end up pregnant and in jail after twelve long years of hard work.

Ever since my sister's funeral, I had partied with the best of them. And, like the rest of the world, I had my own vices. It was hard to accept and take full responsibility for my actions. I continued to justify stabbing Boomquifa, but as I laid in bed in that cell most nights, I only wished I'd used a better way to resolve the conflict I had with her.

The only remnants left from graduation day were my cap and gown still encased in plastic, a few autographs, name cards in my senior memory book, and some letters from my guardian of supporters. I received many letters from my mom, a cheerleading advisor, a few friends, teachers, and a school administrator. Over the next several months, these letters became something to look forward to. Each letter was like having a slice of my grandfather's pound cake. Only inmates can honestly relate to the power of the pen and the sheer excitement that consumes and recharges the spirit with each letter received.

A few days after the graduation ceremony, I received a card that had a vibrant, multicolored frog, hanging on a red flower and green stem. The artist framed the picture on the card in such a way, I had to imagine or guess the exact type of flower from which the colorful frog was hanging. The background of the photo was green, and I could only infer that the photographer took this picture in the frog's natural habitat. In a blank card, my Challenge English teacher wrote:

Dear Keturah, June 10, 1996

I was sorry to hear about all your troubles and thought about you yesterday at graduation. My grandmother used to say that everything was for the best, so maybe something good can come out of all of this. Stay positive!

How's the pregnancy going? Mrs. Grant keeps me informed somewhat, and she gave me this address. If you'd like to write to me, I'd like it as well.

I hear you've been writing. Good! You know how I feel about the value of writing to clean out the mind and soul. Well, I'll try to visit some weekend if they let me.

Keep strong,
Mrs. Eddington

#

My mother wrote:

June 16, 1996

Hello,

How are you doing? Have any of your cousins or friends written to you? Keturah, these moments are when you'll realize who cares about you.

When we lost your sister, her death made me realize who was truly there for me. Her death showed me the true hearts and character of my siblings, as well as, my friends. You'll realize most people are only around when you can be of use to them. So, when you come home, it's time to let them go.

I'm praying you'll get an early release. To have you home again, will be the happiest day of my life. We'll have a cookout and a baby shower combined to celebrate your early release.

I've enclosed some more stamps, put $25 on your books, sent writing paper, and a bar of soap, so, let me know if you don't get them. That should keep you going for a while. If you need anything, just let me know. If they don't let you have the grease, I'll go out and find some that you can.

Well, I'm ending this letter, so, be strong because we want you home!

Love always,
Mom

#

A letter from my cheerleading advisor read:

June 20, 1996

Dear Keturah,

I'm sorry I haven't been able to contact you earlier. I don't know if Phil told you, but I just moved to California. I know you tried to call me quite a bit, it

Grandpa's Pound Cake

always seems to me on the days when I have one million things to do. Other days, I was home all day, I kept hoping you will call, but you didn't.

Anyway, I am in California now - I moved on the fourteenth, I have a little more time to get some of the important things done like writing to you! - That I have been putting off.

I am so sorry to hear about what happened to you. It makes me sick to my stomach to think of you in jail. I get so angry when I hear about all those people who commit horrible crimes and spend little or no time in jail. Then, someone like you, who has so much potential, must sit in a detention center. I know you will do your best to make sure you can get into the facility where they will let you keep your baby.

When I was in Mr. Mead's room the other day, I was looking through all the cheerleading pictures. I found a great one of you from camp with your hair in braids. You are not wearing your cheer uniform so it's probably one of those times; you guys were getting ready to go out. It's a great picture - I framed it and put it in my living room.

Keturah, I hope you know how much I enjoyed having you on the squad. Even when you were a pain in the ass, you were one of my favorites. I couldn't say a lot of things to you guys because I had to be professional. I know people thought I played favorites. That's not true. Yes, certain girls, I liked more, but it certainly wasn't because you guys always did what I asked.

The real reason I liked you guys so much is when you weren't telling me what you weren't going to do you worked hard. And I knew deep down you guys respected what I had to do, even if you push the limits all the time. When you guys didn't like what I did, you told me. You didn't make your parents come in and cuss me out or yell at me. I appreciated that.

So enough about all that - I'm glad I was the advisor because I got to meet people like you and the girls on your squad. You guys made it fun. I got tired of you guys telling me I was wrong though. But we did have fun especially during your junior year - I think that was the best of the three.

Oh, by the way, I am no longer Mrs. Manukgan. I changed my name back to my maiden name Myers, much easier huh. I know I am going to like it here in California. I was tired of Columbus. I wasn't going to coach cheerleading anymore and I needed a new job, so here I am. I am going to be teaching middle school kids with behavioral disorders. That should be interesting, huh?

Okay, so now what happens with you? Phil said they will move you to Cleveland when a bed is open. He said you will move thereafter the baby's born so you could be together. I know you, Keturah. I know you make yourself physically sick with stress. I hope you are trying to take care of yourself for your baby's sake. You must eat and try to think positively. I wrote a letter to the Judge for you.

I hope it will help. I know when you are in the middle of something terrible, it is hard to see anything good, but you must try. Otherwise, you may get depressed and lose the part of you we all love. If you lose your self-esteem, your energy, and your excitement for life; then they have won, and you have loss. I know you won't put up with that!

Are you still writing poetry? You'd better be. You're so good at it, please don't give it up. I think of you every time I get my pictures developed because you are so talented and creative in photography. I don't want to make it sound as if I think what you are going through is not difficult. I know that it is. But I also know you and I are alike in that we are survivors.

You guys know me as a coach, but you didn't see many of the things I went through in my private life. You are in a difficult place for a while, but it is not the end of your life. I thought my divorce would kill me, but it didn't. It made me a better, stronger person. This will make you better and stronger if you let it.

People out here love you, please don't forget that! You're having a baby that needs you. I don't know whether you believe in God, but I do. I'm not one of those people who go around blabbing about God and what he can do for you, but I do know he has never let me go through something I wasn't strong enough to handle. I think about you so often and hope you're okay. If you need to talk, you can still call me collect after 5 PM would be great. If not, that's fine too.

Take care of yourself. If you need anything, let me know. Please write to me if you can. I will try to write again soon. I don't know what you want to call me since my name is different.

With love,
Ms. Myers

#

In a second envelope, Ms. Myers wrote:

Hello, I hope all is well. I'm not sure if you remember completing this "Who am I" exercise I assigned to each cheerleader at the beginning of the year - I came across yours and thought you might read it for inspiration, and to remind yourself of who you are.

I continued reading, what looked more like a draft of incomplete thoughts thrown together in an unfinished assignment:

Who am I? I'm straightforward and strong-willed.

I'm the captain of my cheerleading team. I don't like people who misuse power. I don't like getting up early in the morning. I have lots of self-esteem. I like dim lights and being alone in my room. I love money, I hate cowards, and I love privacy. I'm the eldest of my mother's two children. I was raised in a single-parent household most of my life, which has made me a stronger, independent, self-confident person. I'm a loving, caring person who's protective when necessary. These are the requirements I'm convinced will make me a successful person.

I value many things, such as social equality, nature, life, and personal space. I'm a private person. Being the captain of my squad, I've learned the qualities to become a better person. I've learned more about self-control, compromise, and leadership. I've also served as the lab manager for the last two years in the photography program at the career center. My goal is to be a photojournalist. I decided to work towards my vocational certificate, rather than my college prep certificate hoping to get a head start on my career. This is who I am.

#

The truth of the matter regarding settling for a vocational certificate was I hated my French teacher. She and I were archenemies, and to make matters worse, she was the only teacher in the entire school who taught French. I needed those credits to earn a college prep diploma, which was important to me. However, it didn't help, when I found myself lost in the language of love and at a point of no return. Instead of asking for help, I sat in the classroom looking out the window daydreaming, which aggravated the hell out of my teacher.

One day she was so furious that I was staring out the window at the long private driveway lined with big tall fluffy trees, complementary to the green fields of Brookhaven High School's property. She stomped over and stood between the windows and me. I honestly never saw her coming. I was too focused on concentrating on my daydream. She angrily pulled down all the shades to the windows. It bothered me none, and I continued to stare at the shades as if she never shut them.

She walked over with her eyes bulging and her face red, she ordered me to sit in the back of the classroom. I stood my ground and refused to budge. I let her know, I refused to sit in the back of anybody's classroom. Though I may go through life wishing I'd received my college prep certificate, as opposed to the basic graduation diploma, I decided I had to live with it. This was one lesson I was learning well.

8 MY SISTER THE LEGEND

I rubbed my stomach and remembered when I begged my mother for a little sister. My mother said, "Girl go on somewhere, I ain't havin' no more babies." One day she told me she was having a baby. For a long time, I believed my mother had my sister because I asked for her. I didn't discover the truth until I was old enough to understand the birds and the bees.

My sister was born in 1984 when I was seven. My mother says my sister and I were both premature babies. My sister was born three months early and stayed in the hospital in the first four months of her life. We lived on Hamlet Street in the Short North, a low-income area. My mom didn't own a vehicle, nor did she know how to drive at that time. She and I walked to visit my sister at the Ohio State University Hospital. I stood on my tiptoes to look at my sister in the incubator. I couldn't wait for her to come home to join our family. I was happy to have a sister and not be the only child.

I loved and missed my sister dearly. Her battle with cancer and my memories of her battle the incurable disease haunted me. She is a happy memory, but the memory of her fighting to live while dying was painful. She was a spirited little fighter; comedic, blunt with her words, and I adored her. My mom loved my sister too. She once told me that she loved my sister more than she loved me because she explained that I left her. However, I didn't leave her; Lucifer raped me, and that experience forced me to make a difficult decision for myself, and I chose to protect myself. But I never left her, as she stated.

One night my mom woke me up by flicking my bedroom lights on and screaming in a panic. "Get up! Let's go! Get dressed!" I opened my eyes and the yellow lights bounced from the walls back to my eyes. My mom's tone startled me. She threw a jogging suit on my bed and I put it on. When I walked out of my bedroom, the paramedics were carrying my sister to the ambulance. I heard one of them say my sister's temperature was 103.7. My mom told them she tried to get her temperature down but couldn't. This was our first scary experience with my sister's health.

I laid there in my cell and thought about how life was unfair. Years earlier, my sister's diagnosis with rare cancer called Neuroblastoma, caused her death. Neuroblastoma is a type of cancer that affects children 6 and under. When my sister died, I died a little too. Life was pushing me deeper into a dark pit each time a tragic event happened. Thinking about my sister dying made me sad. And it scared me knowing there was a possibility my child could suffer from a terminal illness. The doctors don't know if Neuroblastoma is hereditary, nor do they know where it comes from. It made me nervous about being pregnant.

My sister fought the incurable disease for over two years. She and my parents traveled back-and-forth to San Francisco, Cincinnati, and Cleveland for experimental drug treatments, not covered by our insurance, nor were the treatments guaranteed to make my sister better. My mom, Phil, our family, and the community put in work and made a compassionate effort to raise money for my sister's treatment. We sold soul food, chicken dinners, and had benefit drawings.

My sister, my mom, Phil and I made a couple of appearances on our local news stations, - and Ohio's Black Newspaper "The Call and Post" wrote articles to raise money and awareness of my sister fighting to live. And, I'll never forget the toy spree my sister went on. I helped her place the top of the line toys in the shopping cart as we raced through Toys R' Us. She got a Super Nintendo with some games, a motorized gray jeep, a blue and white table set for kids, a pair of rollerblades with a helmet and kneepads to match, and, much more.

I don't remember the last time I saw my sister alive. It appears when I was beginning to live my sister was dying. Before my sister's death, my mother sent me to visit with my Aunt Harriet in Hawaii. I remembered getting on the plane, but don't remember the last time I saw my sister. I didn't understand that the last time I saw her, was my last time seeing her.

My parents expected my sister to take a turn for the worse, so, my mother, Phil, and my Aunt Harriet decided to remove me from that experience. Following the latest social cues and trends of society, as well as, helping to commercialize my experience, this act didn't help me to come to grips with my sister's death. It isolated me from her when she needed me most. I needed to be with her.

Americans prefer to tuck the image, reminder, and experience of death and old age away from society, making it an abstract phenomenon. When the elderly or a loved one becomes ill, it's customary to send them to a hospital or nursing home to live out their lives and die, making the experience sad and lonely.

My mother remembers when it was customary for people to hold funerals in their house. She remembers going to the funeral of her maternal great grandmother, in the living room of her maternal great grandmother. She recalls the details of her great-grandmother laying in a casket in front of a big window. She was old and laid in the casket, on top of her long, black hair, deeply rooted in her Indian heritage. My mom said her experience with death wasn't scary; it felt normal.

The sick and elderly used to die at home. But, to create the illusion and notion that we've preserved the fountain of youth, nowadays, we send people to hospitals to die in a formal stark environment. I imagine dying at home would be better, in a familiar place, around familiar people, and around the people and things that bring magic to one's life. Things that give the feeling of nostalgia; like the smell of your house, the feel of the carpet, the warmth of your home, intimate family photos, and your favorite chair, make dying less painful.

If it's true that our ancestors are waiting for loved ones on the other side, I'd say, it's more fitting for immediate family and friends to gather on this living side to send off dying loved ones. Wouldn't that be a happier moment? One celebrated family member being sent off to other celebrated family members, joyously awaiting to receive them. This is probably the greatest support one can provide to another human being, giving comfort and love to loved ones until they reach the other side. Those sentiments are important in life, most important in the end. We've allowed society to turn customs surrounding dying from an intimate moment into a formal one - a commercialized experience.

I wasn't given a choice when I was sent to Hawaii,

nor was I told the severity of my sister's health; so, I didn't have enough information to make an informed decision. When I traveled to Hawaii, I didn't know my sister's finale was coming. Had I known my sister was going to die while I was away, I would have chosen to stay by her side. Children are more resistant than most realize. I vividly remember the moment I found out my sister died.

I was in Hawaii for about two weeks. I didn't have much time to explore the island. Most of my time there, my aunt and uncle were working, and my cousin was doing whatever it is that he did. My first weekend there, my aunt took me driving around Waikiki. It was a beautiful island; the sky seemed to be closer to the earth. My aunt swore that though I don't like coconut, I would love the fresh coconut plucked off the tree. On our way to the beach, she pulled over and bought a fresh coconut from a man selling them on the side of the road. My taste buds weren't convinced there was any difference between coconuts I tasted in the past compared to the fresh coconut we'd purchased on a narrow road on Waikiki Island.

Going to the beach and to the movies were the only two activities that broke up the monotony of my two weeks in Hawaii. That weekend, the four of us went downtown to the big movie theater and on a gigantic screen, we saw, "What's Love Got to With It." Actress Angela Bassett gave the performance of her lifetime portraying Tina Turner. Tina Turner's story greatly impacted me, and I was impressed with Angela's physical transformation; her biceps demanded the attention of the audience. Tina Turner's story reminded me of my mother's volatile relationship with Lucifer. I hoped that I would never experience a relationship with a man that would make me question what love has to do with it.

One day the phone rang, and soon after, my aunt came to the guest room. I looked up at her; she didn't have to say anything. I fell to the floor broken. My sister was gone, and I was devastated. I went to my cousin's bedroom, fell to his floor, and just cried. My parents delayed the funeral for four days, due to my aunt and me traveling from Hawaii to Columbus, Ohio.

We arrived in Columbus on the day of the funeral. When I walked into the house, an overwhelming feeling of death came over me. I could hardly breathe because the energy in the house was so different. I felt my sister's presence was no longer with me. I was alone and an only child again. I cried nonstop. At the funeral, I couldn't look at my sister's distorted body in the small casket. I tried to look, but I turned away. Cancer and fluid put so much pressure on her brain; it caused her eyes and forehead to protrude. I didn't want to remember my sweet little sister like that.

Watching as she transitioned out of this world, and knowing my sister's body and mind were deteriorating, was like witnessing, her light slowly dimming and quietly shutting off. I often caught her staring off into space, maybe high off the morphine that stabilized her pain. Sometimes, she'd stare into space with her lips moving; it appeared as if she was somewhere else talking to someone. I would sometimes feel startled by the movements of her lips, the quiet of her tongue, and her deep focal stare into space. And whatever kept her alive, before drying out her bones until she became brittle, simultaneously quieting her mind before her last breath, did the same with the rest of the family – making us quiet and empty, as well.

In a way, my pregnancy was like my experience with my sister's death. The two experiences differed in that with my sister's death, I was the observer. As the observer, Time had less of an effect on me; but because my sister and I shared a bond, our hearts, and blood connected, Times forces, strongly weighed me down.

I was forced to step outside of myself and slow my life journey down, so I could clearly focus and experience life scene by scene, giving me the ability to hear differently too. My Aunt Harriet didn't have to form the message of my sister's loss on her tongue. I felt it, saw it, and heard it without my aunt saying anything. In a strange way, my sister's death gave me the gift of hearing through vibes, no need to speak words or use gestures.

My second lesson in life was learning to hear. The first was watching my mom and Phil grieve as my sister withered away. My mom's nerves got so bad that we made a rule as a family that we wouldn't call her on her job. Every time she got a call, she feared the worse. This made her a nervous wreck, always anticipating the final call. That's exactly why I knew someone calling, and my aunt coming to my room meant she wouldn't be delivering happy news.

This explains why somethings such as vanity becomes less important to those who are ill or dying. In that state, most don't care what other people think? My sister never did. She refused to wear a wig, and this was before the days of the bald cancer head becoming a statement. My sister didn't let the culture of hair define her. She didn't care what other people thought. Hair makes us feel beautiful, helps to define our personality, social status, age, wealth, rank, and marital status amongst other visual descriptions. My sister knew exactly what defined her.

As I witnessed my sister's spiritual journey, her losing her hair, and becoming completely bald, she was courageously confident at 8 years old. She tried wearing a wig, hated it, and refused to wear one. She existed proudly without her hair. She was more beautiful for it. She was a youthful example to the rest of the world. Her baldhead represented confidence.

My sister was able to look at and accept herself

without a drop of culture to define herself. She was wise to know the only way to truly define oneself is to look beneath the hair and the natural bald canvas to see what's on the inside. Maybe my sister was forced to step outside of herself to see herself for who she was before leaving this place. The balding journey tends to bring on such experiences.

For those who've come close to death and attempt to hold on to human vanity, in my opinion, they truly have not yet come close enough to death. Many who are close to death lose their filter that once funneled their consideration of other people's existence. This seems to die an early death, so those close to death can conserve their energy and time before dying. These experiences teach us how to truly be free.

My sister was my first experience with death. I used to think the world stopped when people died. Through my blurry, puffy, tear-filled eyes; I was surprised to see people laughing and smiling, even my extended family. I couldn't force myself to smile or laugh. I couldn't make myself do anything but cry. I didn't feel like anyone cared that she died, except my parents and me.

I remembered my cousin explaining that everyone takes their last shit shortly after their last breath. She explained my grandmother's belief that putting on clean underwear before dying was a waste of time because we all die with shit in our pants. My sister's death reminded me of this childhood conversation, which reminded me of a time my cousins, sister, and I was altogether. My sister asked my eldest cousin to pull her finger. When my cousin pulled her finger, my sister farted. My cousin must have smelled it because she advised my sister to check her underpants. Sho'nuff, she'd shitted her pants.

We come in this world shitting and we die shitting. The same sentiments go for the pain we experience in our lifetime. Most come in this world in pain, and most of us die in pain. This must be what the phrase hell on earth means. Most spend a lifetime reliving the same experience, trying to learn a single lesson in life, meanwhile, reliving a painful experience we can't correct. That must be hell on earth.

Anticipating my sister jumping out from her favorite hiding place, a corner in the house where she liked to jump out and scream, "Boo!" scared me for a while. Being in our bedroom with the memories we shared was also suffocating. I couldn't bring myself to sleep there. I was too scared to close my eyes, especially at night. Before my sister died, sleeping in the dark didn't bother me. After she died, I slept with the light or TV on for a while.

My best friend Ava and her mother were compassionate and allowed me to stay with them for a couple of weeks. After the funeral, my house was cold, empty, and heavy. I cried and cried. The thought of my sister in the cold, dark grave by herself, tormented my psyche. I didn't want my sister to be alone, not even in death.

We held my sister's funeral on July 3, 1993, which fell on a Friday that year. After the funeral, my boyfriend at the time had a big party. I didn't want to go, but Ava's mom persuaded me to go. She told me, "You can't stop living because someone dies; you have a long life to live. Let this make you strong, not weak."

I figured she knew what she was talking about since she'd lost a son to cancer. I wanted to be strong but didn't have any strength left; kind of like I felt laying in that cell, helpless, weak, and vulnerable. I went to the party and hit the blunt every time it rolled around. At the end of the night, I was drunk, high, and numb; but my entire being still hurt. I missed my sister painfully.

After her death, for years I'd have similar reoccurring dreams about my sister. In those dreams, she was always dead. Sometimes, her body was like a stuffed animal, like the ones we won at the state fair. In those dreams, it was obvious we worshiped her; because, we placed her on a dresser or counter on display.

These disturbing dreams occurred so often that I eventually had to pray to God for him to take the dreams away from me. I prayed that my sister could no longer enter my dreams. The last dream I had of her was of the two of us in our bedroom sitting on a bed. She was older and so was I, and we were happily conversing as sisters do. I woke up from that dream feeling happy, as though my sister visited me in person. I believe that was her way of letting me know she is in a better place.

When someone dies and a loved one can't visualize the face of their beloved, the misplaced memories can cause stress. Questions go through your mind like, why can't I remember what they looked like, am I selfish, should I keep living, do I deserve to live, why should I live? This experience can sometimes cause feelings of survivor's guilt. Death is a mind fuck anyway. If you think deeply about death, you'll realize, no matter what, death wins.

Religion advises us not to question things we don't understand or can't explain. Overthinking and worrying can cause us to think ourselves into a black hole filled with mental illness. That's why anything unexplainable and/or permanent can be scary because it's an uncontrollable, unchangeable entity. The permanence of death and the fear of the unknown scare many into complacency and stagnation. Living a careful life, hoping Death can't find us, or some other powerful entity will. But even if we stand still, Time continues to move and so does Death, or that other entity will. No matter what we do, Death or that other entity still comes and there's nothing we can do but accept it.

Time is relative and yes, my sister's life was short. Who can define or measure another's life? I believe my sister is the only one that can measure her time here on earth. Although young, she was wise. She told Phil on her deathbed that she was ready. Throughout her young life, she impacted many lives. Only those who have been close to death understand that seconds get longer the sicker and closer death gets to you; time slows until it stops. One philosophy I believe is that the painful experience is so great, so we'll want to leave our bodies. Otherwise, without experiencing pain, some people would never leave their bodies or this world.

Being in a room when someone's heart stops and their soul leaves the room it becomes awkwardly peaceful. This experience is like no other. American society perforated the idea of death and removed death from the social experience to sell the idea of morality, which most find more attractive.

Unspoken Expression

I suppose I'll never get over the death of my sister. Over the years, I've discovered that the older one gets, the more important siblings become. I've watched other people and their siblings, and I've observed how they interact and treat one another. I've observed the good, the bad, and the ugly in their relationships. However, ultimately the support, companionship, and love that these siblings provide to each other are priceless. The true impact siblings have on each other's lives isn't measurable or measured until one of them dies, a good example of life's teachings. Death teaches us how significant people are to our own existence and how important our existence is to others.

It's quite lonely being an only child. Sure, there's the benefit of being spoiled. But at the end of the day, for me, the materialistic items didn't make me rich. I've witnessed siblings literally hating the other and going as far as wishing the other dead. I often find myself envious of their opportunity to one day see and speak to their sibling again. Just having the opportunity sometimes leads the quarreling siblings into believing their false reality; time and death doesn't wait for the stubborn hearted forgivers.

To this day, I carry the memory of my sister around with me because she's still a big part of who I am. When I introduce myself, shortly after, or maybe months later, I'll soon introduce my sister into the conversation. I'm sure; I don't have an acquaintance, that doesn't know that I have a deceased sister. Talking about her is the only way to keep the memory of her alive.

Death isn't something to get over. Like every other traumatic life experience, I learned to cope with my sister's death. I still process the big why her? Why die at that time? Why die like that? I've listened to the explanations of superstitious people, Christian people, and everybody else in between, and all people have their own perspective and theory as to why God calls children home. I've never found any answers, nor comfort, from any of the theories I've heard thus far. I would like to believe that my sister was assigned to a short assignment. I would like to believe that she greatly impacted many lives and was called home early. I rebuke the idea that my mother did something so bad that God chose to take my sister as punishment.

9 SPADES TOURNAMENTS

Occasionally, the staff at Scioto had spades tournaments that were kind of fun. The tournaments broke up the monotony of our day. The tournaments took place on Saturdays as a treat to the girls who weren't on restriction. The staff would give out Ramen Noodles as a reward. Those Ramen Noodles were special, and they tasted extra special in there.

My pregnant partner and I sat at a table across from the opposing team. My family believes pregnant people are lucky; and, I felt lucky too. At that time, my brain was sharp. I could count and memorize every card played. We got down to the last hand. One of the other girls from the other team threw a card that they had already played, and they won the tournament. They rejoiced with my teams Ramen Noodles. My partner and I both knew they'd cheated. Neither one of us made a fuss about it though; it wasn't a big deal; it was just the principal of the matter. The other two girls were juvenile lifers, and they probably needed those Ramen Noodles more than we did.

After the fun and games were over, a guard came to our cottage, pulled my spades partner to the side, and told her that her kid's father was shot and killed. She told us they denied her request to attend the funeral of her unborn child's father. She was devastated and cried for days. I felt so sorry for her.

One event took place after another in Scioto. The boys sent there stayed in a cottage on the other side of the property. I'd heard, the boys housed at Scioto were sick, diseased, or had some type of mental problem. One day, two boys escaped through a hole in the fence. They immediately locked down the entire facility. As a result of the lockdown, they locked all of us in our cells for the next 24 hours; we even ate our meals there.

I sat in my cell all evening and drowned in misery. My arms were limp and my body restless. The four walls were tight. I wanted to jump out of my skin. Being stuck in the cell was so unnatural. I was inflicted and unbalanced in my being. I resented not having control over anything. For the first time, I realized how completely powerless I was.

By the next evening, after they found the boys that escaped, things went back to normal. We were able to have dinner in the dining hall. The moment the phone was free, I phoned home to Jacob, who was surprisingly supportive. I'd always assumed that if I got pregnant, the father wouldn't stick around; my father didn't. I could count on my hands how many times I'd seen my biological father. I, therefore, figured that Jacob wouldn't be around for my pregnancy; I assumed he'd be a deadbeat like my biological father.

Scioto's rules didn't permit Jacob to visit me, but he supported me the only way that he could. That meant everything to me. Only my immediate family could visit, so he waited at my house almost every day for my call. Talking to him was a positive force that kept me halfway in the game.

I felt guilty that the father of my child wanted to be a part of my baby's life and was unable to do so because I got myself locked up. I thought it ironic though that society normalized the idea of black fathers in jail in the 90s, I never realized how many women were doing time, I didn't know any. My idea of fatherhood was a product of my environment. Many of my fellow Generation X'ers that I grow up with, some of my good friends, some ex-boyfriends, and a few cousins, spent time in and out of jail; mostly for selling crack cocaine. Some of our mindsets and our ideas were just as broken as the homes in which we grew up. Many Generation X'ers were broken for many reasons related to being the seeds of the crack epidemic.

Some kids I grew up with raised themselves. I saw it with my own eyes. Kids getting themselves to middle school or running households because their parents were too high and lost somewhere out in the world. The 80s and 90s were rough for people. I was fortunate that my mom was never a crackhead or used any form of drugs. That's not to say that crack cocaine didn't touch my family or affect people close to me.

Looking into the environment I grew up in, and the one my friends grew up in, are some of the reasons it's important to me that my child's father plays an active role in the life of our child.

#

One late rainy night during my last month at Scioto, two guards dragged in a girl who went by the name of Fatama. She looked like a wet, black puppy dog. I was under the assumption she came in on a parole violation. It was the first time I'd seen anyone come in at night. I stared at the girl through the small, rectangle-shaped window. She had a dark complexion with raccoon-like eyes that were almost black; and, her hair was short, nappy, and wet, sticking straight up on her head. It was obvious the girl was pregnant. I could easily see her baby bump, as it protruded through her dingy-looking shirt, and she could hardly zip up her jeans that were covered in mud.

Fatama was only there for two days before she was

flirting with gay activity. When she kissed her girlfriend Terri, it was the first time I'd ever seen two girls kissing with tongue. I found it weird because she was pregnant. Fatama had to be the product of some insane society. The rumor was that she kissed coochies on the ins and was strictly dickly on the outs. I don't think it mattered where she was, she conducted herself loosely.

She had a big mouth too and was so pregnant that she couldn't tie her shoes. Everybody knew she liked her girlfriend Terri to tie her shoes for her. I thought Fatama was a whiny little attention seeker. Fortunate for us pregnant girls, her whining paid off. As a result, of her whining, the pregnant girls got a double scoop of food.

I couldn't believe Fatama went into the meeting and told the staff, "I be hoon-gry. Terri gives me her food, but I still be hooon-gry. And I'm hooon-gry right now." I laughed at how she put an o in hungry and stressed the O. It was funny, and it's still funny now. She was ghetto fabulous and knew how to get us extra food.

The other girls told me a story about a pregnant girl who was there prior to my incarceration. They said, the girl was sick and requested to go to the hospital, but the guards denied her request. They said that when the girl went into labor, her baby was stillborn; and, because staff failed to provide her medical treatment, she sued the state and received an early release. They also said that's why the pregnant girls have so many meetings, to make sure they meet all our needs. Three other pregnant girls, including Fatama and me, had several meetings throughout my two months or so at Scioto, with Fatama being our ghetto fabulous advocate.

Bloody Ink

One peaceful and quiet night, I fell asleep and woke up with the baby resting on my bladder; my lower abdomen ached. I badly needed to use the restroom, so I got up and knocked on the small window of my cell to get the COs attention. I knocked and knocked, but no one came to relieve me. Something was going on in the cell next to mine. Ashley had a single bunk cell and I watched the guards go back and forth and in and out of her room several times. Something had happened to her, but I didn't give a dang what it was because I had to pee. I peeked through the window trying to see, what I could see. From the angle from where I was looking, I could hardly see anything.

My stomach ached and I had to pee. I continued to knock on the window of my cell door and the guards pissed me off because nobody came. When I arrived at Scioto, Ashley was on suicide watch that night too. During my time at Scioto, she was on suicide watch so many times that I lost count. At that moment, all I wished for was for Ashley to get her wish. "Let her die!" I thought to myself, "I have to pee!" I figured that if Ashley wanted to kill herself, she would've gotten it right by now. I saw Ashley being wheeled out of her cell. She laid on a medical bed lifeless, her eyes shut, hair matted, and, her white skin had turned pale blue. I watched the nurse wheel her out of my point of sight.

The CO walked to the rectangle-shaped window and told me to wait a couple more minutes, so they could clear the place. As soon as the nurse and Ashley left, they let me out. The cottage was quiet. I was curious as I passed Ashley's cell, so I took a long peek to see what Ashley had done. I saw Ashley's name and birthdate written in giant bloody letters on the wall. She must have cut herself bad to draw enough blood to write her name that big. After I peed, I went back to my cell and slept like a baby for the rest of the night.

#

The next morning, two other girls and I had a doctor's appointment at the Ohio State University Hospital's OBGYN clinic. I would've never figured that the state juvenile prison system, took pregnant inmates to a regular doctor's office off-campus. I didn't expect it. The other two girls and I lined up and followed the CO down the path to the fancy lobby with the big glass windows. Before we left, the guards handcuffed and shackled the other inmates and me. I was experiencing cultural shock all over again. I couldn't believe I was pregnant, handcuffed, and shackled. We looked and sounded like a rap song. One guard walked in front of us and another walked behind us, as they led us to the white van used to transport us to our medical appointments.

We wore loose white shirts and gray jogging pants with the letters O.D.Y.S. going down the sides. For those of us fortunate enough to have nice sneakers, the other inmates considered us fashionable in that joint. New shoes were a link to the outside world and a status symbol. One earned respect when they looked good, at least to others on the outside looking in; the person appeared to have mastered a form of happiness in Scioto. We didn't look that bad, but the handcuffs and shackles stood out like rejected jewelry pieces.

The clinic was in the main hospital. When we arrived, I sat down and made sure I sat with good posture and crossed my feet, so the shackles weren't so obvious. I tried not to look so pitiful. I was ashamed that I was in jail and didn't want anyone seeing me escorted by guards. I never liked people putting me on the spot; the light was not only bright but also hot.

A nurse walked the girls and me to the back where the rooms were located. While I stood with one of the other girls waiting for my room, I saw my neighbor's older cousin. She had been at the scene on the day of the stabbing. Wow! What a coincidence!

She had the pleasure of seeing me in handcuffs and shackles. I was furious and humiliated that the cousin got the double satisfaction of seeing me in chains. When the guard unlocked my feet, I followed the nurse to the room. I wanted to take the footrest of the bed off, go find that bitch, and beat the shit out of her for the double insult. I thought that's how I got in this situation in the first place. It only took a moment of lapsed judgment to change my life forever.

Nevertheless, I couldn't find any outlet for my anger. My arms throbbed with anger, as it pulsated through my hands. I was so mad but couldn't release it. I always kept the thought of an early release in the back of my mind and used those thoughts to bargain with myself. The thought of an early release was my tongue and my minds keeper.

The nurse asked me if I was having any problems. I told her about the constant spitting and heartburn I was having. It was so bad the acid refluxed and traveled all the way up to the back of my ear tubes. The nurse took my vital signs, gave me a gown, told me to undress from the waist down, and that the doctor would be in shortly. The doctor was concerned about my diet but understood I had no control over what I ate. All he told me was to stay away from foods that contained any types of acids like tomatoes, lemons, orange juice, and things acidic in nature.

The doctor also gave me permission to have as much Maalox as needed. It was the next best way to keep me comfortable, considering my pregnancy condition. Because I couldn't swallow my saliva, there was nothing to coat the acid in my stomach, thus, resulting in heartburn from hell, in addition to spitting up mucus and the vomiting that accompanied it.

There was only one occasion at Scioto where a male nurse that frequently worked the night shift, refused to give me Maalox. After I reported the incident to my mother, and my attorney contacted Scioto, I never had any other problems. The doctor performed a pap smear and performed an ultrasound. I watched in amazement as the doctor pointed out that I was having a little girl. At that moment, I wished Jacob were there at my side to share that moment with me.

The nice guard that escorted us kept the handcuffs and shackles off while I waited in the waiting room for the other two girls. I got stares from the other patients, and it made me feel uncomfortable. I never wanted people to see me or think of me as a bad person. That doctor's appointment changed me forever. The unnatural spirit of caring what others think of me infected me at a great level and stayed with me for most of my young adult years. At such times in a person's life, they shouldn't care what others think of them. But there I was, eighteen and forced to examine every aspect of my life.

As we left the hospital, I stared out the window at the Ohio State University campus. We rode past students, most likely attending summer school, and I wished I were there; the incoming class of 1996. I won't lie; I was envious of the student's happily walking and smelling freedom.

I closed my eyes and let the wind caress my face through the small opening of the window. The warm sun shined through the window of the van warming the parts of my face that were highlighted. Though I'd been humiliated, being in society for half of a second was exhilarating.

I inhaled as much freedom as I could before the guards drove us back to the dungeon. My eyes were like a minicomputer saving all the positive images: the smiles on people's faces; the green grass; the blue skies, and all the beautiful flowers I saw. These images were powerful, like getting a hug from God, equivalent to pellets in a Pac Man game.

10 PERSPECTIVE

I laid on my bottom bunk and thought of all the crazy crimes that got the other girls convicted. For the most part, most of their crimes were petty. I tried not to be judgmental either way – how could I be? Consequently, I'd never imagined I'd be in an environment with convicted murderers. A Judge convicted my second roommate for murder. Courtney was a juvenile lifer. She was a cool chic. It seemed most of the girls that were convicted were in the wrong place at the wrong time.

Courtney and I laid in our bunks and talked about the group session we had participated in earlier that day. One of the group rules stated that everyone in the group had to share their story. The counselor said it was part of our therapy. I stayed at Scioto for two months and got away without telling my story in a group setting. I learned most of the girls were committed for crimes like stealing, running away, selling drugs, robbery, murder, prostitution; or, simply being in the wrong place at the wrong time; or, with the wrong people. My exposure to hardcore lifestyles was limited, compared to many of the experiences of the other girls.

By the time I got to Scioto, Courtney had been there for four years; and had four more years to do. She was 13 when they convicted her of murder. She was with her brother when some bad shit went down, and her brother shot and killed a guy. They both were on the run for a while. Though she didn't do the shooting, she got juvenile life. I thought her situation was sad because she was with her brother at the wrong time and place. She was only 17 and had to stay there until she was twenty-one.

"So, what's your story? - what did you do to get in here?" she asked me.

My story didn't sound so bad after I heard her awful story. At least, my victim lived.

"My neighbors - their fat ass mama, and her two daughters." I got fired up thinking about the situation. My voice and tone turned into its old self. "They moved next-door to me on the L block, and seriously, I don't know how the conflict started. Just like, I told that stupid Magistrate, I had my own friends, so there was no reason I needed to befriend any of them. But I was neighborly."

"Quida was the older sister and Boomquifa was the younger sister. When they moved in, we were cordial; we spoke to each other from time to time. I had my own friends though, so I didn't see any reason to get all chummy with them bitches. I didn't have a problem with Boomquifa; my problem was with Quida.

I don't know why she had a problem with me. That's probably what confused the court. They probably thought I was just going around stabbin' people. The only cause I could think of is, she must've thought I wanted one of the niggas on the block, she was either jealous, or she wanted to be my friend. If she thought I wanted one of her niggas, if she'd asked me, I would have let her know it wasn't that type of party, and the boys on the block were my boys, straight like family. Quida was a dumbass, I heard she let the guys run trains on her ass and shit.

I grew up with those knuckleheads and didn't want any of them like that. Those are the only reasons; I can think for Quida getting all this shit started. Boomquifa and I just got the short end of the stick.

When Quida moved in, she'd sit on the porch with her friends, stare me down, and snicker with her friends. I finally got tired of her disrespectful ways. For a whole year, Quida and I went back-and-forth bickering. Only, she handled it like a bitch, she only had balls when her friends or family were around. I'd walk past her sitting on her porch, gawking and turning her nose up at me; and I'd ask her what's up?

When her friends were around, she had the balls to talk shit. She never had anything to say when she was by herself, except, "Go ahead Keturah" in her whiny voice. I remember one time she was standing on the side of her house with a guy I went to school with. He'd tried to holler at me, but he didn't have a chance. I asked him, "What the hell are you doing with that doggie?" Not only did our schools have a long history of rivalry, but she and I also became intertwined enemies.

Her crackhead mother and her mother's crackhead boyfriend joined in, calling me all kinds of bitches. The only one from that family that liked me was her five-year-old brother. He had a crush on me and used to call me his girlfriend. Poor boy would sneak to wave and talk to me. Shit was crazy for a long time before the shit hit the fan. That family harassed me for over a year.

My mother worked nine to nine, and Phil worked three to eleven. So, I was always home alone. The day before the incident happened, I had to call my mother and youngest Aunt Eve off their job; and they almost got into a fight with Quida's mother and aunt. I thought the situation was resolved, but it only escalated the next day.

The morning all the drama started, I woke up early, running down the stairs into the bathroom. I had to pee. My room is in the attic. I loved my room because of its size; it was gigantic. The only decorative feature I didn't like was the orange paint, which covered the walls and the thirteen steps I climbed to get to my room. The vinyl flooring was just as bad; the tiles were brown, orange, and yellow. But my closet was huge; it went on, and on; one-third the length of my room. It was a nice room; I just hated the colors. I would have killed to be in my orange room at that time, not literally kill." The two of us giggled.

Direct across from my room was Quida's room. It was almost like a dual. She'd turn the volume to her music to the highest notch, and I would turn mines up, raise my window up, and turn my music up louder. One day, I blew out one of my speakers feuding with that tramp. It was hard to prevent what happened because we lived next door to each other, and it was just too hard to avoid confrontations.

That morning, I got up and got dressed by 10:30 am; I was out the door and on my way to the house of my best friend Ava's. As I left the house to get in my car, Quida, her older cousin, and Boomquifa were standing by their car, parked behind mine. As I got into my car, their older cousin looked at me and asked me if I had a problem?

I said, "Yeah bitch, I have a problem!" I gestured and asked her, "What?" with my arms thrown in the air like I was gangsta. They got me fired up! I was ready to fight! Girl, I was ready to throw 'em up! I was about it, 'bout it and they had got me rowdy, rowd-it," I said laughing. Though it was three of them and one of me, I didn't. I hadn't run from anybody since the day Lucifer raped me.

I got tired of running from people a long time ago. I was tired of being a victim and refused to let anyone rape or disrespect me ever again. I lived with my guards up and protected myself by doing what I had to do by-all-means necessary.

Quida stood there with her pregnant stomach poking out and her two peons standing behind her like she was the Terminator.

"Oh, we'll be back," her older cousin said.

I didn't know what to expect. I figured they were all talk, but I decided to arm myself."

"With a gun?" my roommate asked.

"No girl, thank God for that," I prayed.

"Instead of getting in my car, I went back into the house and grabbed a steak knife for protection. I slid it in the inside of the waistline of my shorts. You know, where the boys keep their guns.

I left for Ava's house. I kicked it with my girl for about an hour and went back home. I drove all the way down Cleveland Avenue and busted a right on Loretta Avenue. It was close to 1 o'clock in the afternoon and everybody was on the block. Everybody hung out on the block before mine. Summertime on my block was always live.

I pulled up in what Quida referred to as the "Grape Ape." I heard Quida had given my car that name. I loved my 1985 four-door, Chevy Cavalier. I got it for my 16th birthday and had it painted purple, had some hammer rims, and a pull out too! I had plans to get some good speakers, and only wished for the purple lights to go underneath my car.

I spoke to everybody on the block. Ms. Susan, one of my friend's moms asked me to come to see her. She told me that her daughter was supposed to do her hair but had canceled on her. She said she'd pay me to put a ponytail in her hair. I did my friend's hair all the time, and ponytails are my specialty. Ms. Susan conveniently had everything I needed, so, I told her okay.

I put her ponytail in and cut the hair. I could tell it was going to be the bomb. I looked at her cheap curling iron and I needed a hotter one to get the results I wanted. So, I decided to leave my car and walk down the street to my house, since it was on the next block, about seven houses down.

As I made my way in front of Quida's house, I looked up at the porch and saw Boomquifa sitting on the porch. I looked up at her and she stared down at me. I looked forward and back at her and saw she was stalking me. No one would expect that prior to that day, Boomquifa and I were cordial with one another; and usually spoke to one another. Though we never had words before, I was agitated about what happened earlier with her and her crew. So, I asked her, "What the fuck are you looking at?"

Boomquifa got up from her chair like a big, bad bitch. She stood up at the top of the steps and said, "I'm not going to stand up here, and let you talk to me like you've been talking to my sister."

So, I asked that bitch, "What then?" I had my arms up, letting her know I was down for whatever. She walked off her porch, down the steps, and stood in front of me, sizing me up. She was a few years younger than her sister and me, and, friendlier than Quida. She was about the same height as me, but a fat butterball.

I exposed the knife right away, hoping she'd run away. I lifted my shirt as if I was showing someone, I had a gun on me. This bitch was either bold or just plain stupid because she still wanted to fight me.

We stood face-to-face and I felt her breath on my face. I don't know who swung first. All I know is everything was moving extremely fast.

I pulled the knife out, and as we struggled, I managed to stab her three times. The knife protruded in and out of her flesh – one, two, three times. I stabbed her, in and out, my form like tenderizing raw meat. It was an odd sensation, feeling the knife moving in and out of her flesh.

Next, out of the corner of my eye, I see her fat ass mom come out of the side door and run down the driveway towards where we were fighting. As she was running down the driveway, Quida and their cousin were pulling up beside us. I ran to my house because I wasn't about to get jumped.

Boomquifa held onto her side and showed her mother where she was bleeding. The way Quida and her cousin pulled up, signified a setup. We all got more than we bargained for that day. I unlocked the door, went inside my house, and tossed the knife into the sink. My intentions were to grab my curling iron and head back to Ms. Susan to finish her hair.

Before I realized what was happening, the doorbell rang. Ms. Susan said she saw what happened, so she ran down to the house to check on me. The police had both houses surrounded in a matter of minutes. It was mass chaos on the block. The police walked up to the house and asked me to come with them. They put me in the back of the cruiser, and they allowed me to give Ms. Susan my mother's work number so she could call her and let her know what was going on.

I must've been in the back of that cruiser for hours. To make matters worse, I was on my period and beginning to lose my cool. I had on a sanitary pad that was a soggy mess. I needed to use the restroom, and when I made that request, the officers told me I had no choice but to wait for a female officer to arrive at the scene. After waiting for an hour or so, a female officer arrived and told me she was going to escort me to the closest headquarters, so I could use the restroom.

There were five police cars and a detective's car outside my house, and my mom was pulling up to the scene. My mother said, when she saw the yellow tape around our houses, she thought I'd killed the girl. The ambulance had rushed Boomquifa to the hospital over an hour ago, her lungs collapsed.

Driving to the police headquarters, I listened to the police radio and heard a police dispatcher come over the air and order all available units to report to the United Dairy Farmers store on the corner of Ferris and Cleveland.

Meanwhile, the female officer and I pulled up to the headquarters in a neighborhood known as the Windsor Terrance, a low-income project located about a mile or so from the L block. It wasn't important for me to use the restroom after the officer told me she had to watch me pee. I was not feeling her watching me change that funky ass sanitary pad. I had no idea having someone watch me pull my pants down would become a routine in my life. I had no idea, what I would have to do now.

The officer returned me to the scene of the crime. When we returned, my mother was waiting at the house worried. The detective came and got me out the car, Uncle Gary, an attorney, was standing next to the detective. Uncle Gary wasn't my blood uncle, but he was my Aunt Harriet's best friend. He's the same lawyer that advised my aunt the day I walked to my grandparents' house after Lucifer raped me.

When I saw him, I realized I was in more trouble than I previously believed. When he looked at me, I wanted to cry; I was ashamed too. He and the detective walked me into the house.

Where did you put the knife after you stabbed Boomquifa? the detective asked.

I looked at my mother and Uncle Gary. They both gave me a nod and look of approval to retrieve the weapon. I walked over to the sink and pointed to the knife. The detective gathered the evidence and placed it in a plastic bag. After the officers retrieved the knife, they permitted me to use the bathroom.

The detective determined that I wasn't a risk to anyone and released me to my parents. My mother wasn't mad at me. She knew what had been going on between my neighbors and me. Furthermore, she was happy I didn't kill the girl. I went upstairs and laid on my bed. I didn't know what that day meant to me.

On top of that, I got a call from Ava, thinking I was going to hear a friendly voice. She called to inform me that one of our closest friends was shot and killed on the corner of Ferris and Cleveland. She said that it was all over the news and everything. Coincidentally, it was the same call I heard come over the police radio when I was in the police cruiser. I couldn't believe that shit. The entire day was just one fucked up day, all day long. I'm happy I didn't go to jail right away."

I laid on my bottom bunk and rubbed my 6-month-old belly. "That's how I ended up here. You do know no self-defense law exists in Ohio. For it to be a fair fight, according to Ohio's self-defense law, Boomquifa would've had to bring a knife to the fight too. That's the biggest reason I'm worried about my early release being denied."

11 EUPHRASIA

"I have Keturah Black ready for transportation," the guard said talking to his walkie-talkie.

I sat in the backseat of an unmarked car designed just like a police cruiser. My hands still locked in handcuffs. I rode in the back of the car in silence. I hadn't had much to say for the past two months, and I didn't want to talk to the guard transporting me, either.

I had a big chip on my shoulder and didn't have the energy to be social. I got everything I needed from my mother and didn't need to engage in worthless conversations with anyone else. I acted as if I was doing everyone a favor by blocking my own blessings. I didn't realize communicating with people in a time like that might do me some good.

"Have you ever been to Cleveland before?" The guard broke the silence.

"No."

"Well, it's going to take about two hours for me to get you there."

The guard was being nice, but I didn't want to talk to him. I didn't know if he had an ulterior motive and determined he was guilty by association. He was a part of the system that incarcerated children to generate the economy; thereby providing jobs for guys like him. Me losing my freedom meant job security for him. But I had to admit, the white guy was handsome with his brown hair. His matching brown eyes were pretty, and his muscular physique, attractive.

About one hour outside of Columbus, the guard got off the highway and pulled into a McDonald's parking lot.

"Do you need to use the restroom?" he asked with his deep, soothing voice.

"Yes." He unlocked the cuffs and removed them.

"Now, I'm not supposed to do this, but as long as you keep it to yourself, I'll buy you something to eat."

There wasn't any need for him to wait for my response, because I was nodding my head in agreement before he finished his question.

"What do you want?"

I spoke up quickly, "A sausage, egg, and cheese Mc Muffin, a hash brown, and a cup of water," I added. I wanted to order a pop, but I know that would've aggravated my spitting problem. "Thank you," I said politely. The baby and I were happy to get a tasty treat. This was the best day since they locked me up. The food and traveling along the highway in a free world made it worthwhile. I felt the baby move around in my stomach; we couldn't wait to eat.

I went to the women's restroom and before leaving, took a second look at myself in the long mirror fixed to the wall. I brushed my hands over my two French braids. I'd gotten my hair done once by Scioto's hairstylist, but was letting my hair grow out; so, I just got a shampoo and blow-dry. Everybody warned me about the stylist being scissor happy.

I walked over and stood beside the guard. He was next in line. He ordered our food and we left. He told me he'd leave the cuffs off because he didn't think I'd be any trouble. I savored every inch of the sandwich and hash brown. Besides the Ramen Noodles, which we ordered from the jail store or won in those spades' tournaments, that sandwich was the best food that I'd eaten in almost three months.

About 11 o'clock am, we got off the highway at exit 107. I could see Cleveland's downtown skyline. We drove about seven minutes and pulled up to what looked like an abandoned wing of the back of a hospital; located right across the street from the ghetto. The guard pulled into a parking lot and the signs read Charity Hospital staff parking only. The guard and I walked up to the building that had a massive entranceway. There were two big doors and an archway made of stone with the engraving which read Euphrasia. The buildings face was intimidating. Euphrasia used to be an old nun convent.

The guard rung the bell and we waited. I didn't know what to expect inside the building. I held my bag that contained my personal belongings and some pictures. A short white woman with short dirty blonde hair opened the door. The CO handed the woman some papers and she signed them. The guard said good-bye, turned around, and left. He left me with the feeling of abandonment. He left me with a stranger in a foreign place. Our bond had formed and dissipated as quickly as the sausage, egg, cheese Mc Muffin. He could have at least seen me inside.

"Keturah, I'm Ms. Molly, the director of Euphrasia. I'm going to show you around and introduce you to some people."

I looked around at my surroundings and tried to make something of the place. I couldn't see anything because they kept all the doors to the rooms closed. The only visual that stood out was a picture of a nun hanging on the wall over the entrance.

Ms. Molly walked over and pushed the button to the elevator. The door opened and the two of us stood there with an awkward silence. The elevator squeaked all the way to the second floor; it was a rusty old elevator. I held on to the sides of its walls as it wiggled as it started up slowly. The door opened to the middle of a small room. There was nothing special about that room. The only furniture in there was a chair, a small table, and two large copy machines in the corner. Looking to my left and to my right, in both directions, there were large gray security doors.

Ms. Molly swiped us through the two big gray doors to the right. After we walked through the doors, Ms. Molly stopped at the first small room where a young pretty attractive black woman in her late 20s was sitting on a couch holding a beautiful black chubby baby about 6 months old. Ms. Molly introduced me to Ms. Viola.

"Ms. Viola usually works over here in the morning," Ms. Molly said, now looking at me. I analyzed everyone I met, and she seemed liked she might be okay. It was quiet in the long corridor. There were five rooms facing the east side of the building. The room Ms. Viola and the chubby baby were in was a small recreational room with a TV, VCR, a box of toys, and two love seats.

The dining room came next. In that room were four small tables and five highchairs that lined the wall; and, a silver cart placed perfectly in the corner. The next room was a small kitchen with a small sink, steam table, two big green commercial refrigerators, and a single cabinet on the wall.

Lastly, the restroom was large and had three showers, three sinks, three mirrors, and a washer and dryer standing side by side in one of the corners. On the other side of the privacy wall, stood three toilet stalls, and standing at the gray door and looking straight ahead was the staff's office.

Ms. Molly showed me around and showed me to my room. I was left alone to settle into my room. Ms. Molly seemed nice, but it was too early to tell. My room was the second room from the staff's office. When I walked in my room, there were two twin beds and a crib, and two table desks that pulled down from the wall and divided the room equally. Below each desk was one deep large drawer and in the far corners of both sides of the room was a closet.

The best feature of the room was a window draped with grayish blue curtains. The window provided a view that looked out to the parking lot of the hospital. In the bottom part of the window was a great big air conditioner. I was impressed. My room was a decent room.

I looked down and for the first time in a while, closed my eyes and exhaled, while rubbing my stomach, which was now growing bigger and bigger every day. About an hour passed and I could hear a selection of voices in the hallway on the other side of my closed door. I didn't bother to peek to see who the voices belonged too. I heard doors shut and it was silent again for 20 minutes. Shortly after, the smell of lunch lingered in the air, followed by a knock on my door. An older woman peeked through the door and told me to wash up for lunch.

The bathroom was across from my room, which was convenient for me with all my spitting and peeing all the time. I walked in the bathroom and two of the three girls greeted me. One of the girls was skinny and tall. She had that pretty chubby baby on her hip making her wave hi. The other girl was average in height and on the heavy side with a big donkey booty. She stood in front of the skinny girl playing with the baby.

"This is June and I'm Natalie, but you can call me Natie," the skinny girl said introducing the baby and herself.

"And I'm Daytona," the other girl said.

"I'm Keturah," I said as I washed my hands and followed the other girls to the dining room.

At one of the tables was a young light-skinned girl sitting with a cute little baby boy about a year old. He looked just like her; they both had long narrow heads and big eyes. She sat at the table feeding him with one hand and had two of her fingers in her mouth.

The older lady who called us for lunch pushed in the silver cart with plates of food on the top of the cart and a big bowl of salad on the bottom. A row of bowls was stacked next to the salad. We said our grace, made our plates, and everyone ate.

"Where you from?" Daytona asked while dipping her turkey in her potatoes and gravy.

"Columbus."

"When are you due?" the young girl asked with her two fingers still in her mouth.

"October 26, two days after my birthday," I announced.

"How old are you?" Natalie asked.

They were a friendly group of girls, but nosey.

"18," I said. I felt old.

Most of the girls were between the ages of 12-16. Euphrasia was a low-security treatment center that housed up to fifteen girls and five children.

"What are you doing here? You must've gotten lucky," the girl stressed as she put her fingers back in her mouth.

"If that's what you call it," I replied with a combination of a sigh and a huff. "I'm here with Yawl, I guess I'm lucky," I said sarcastically. We all laughed at the dull humor that wasn't that funny.

After lunch, the girls got their children situated and asked the staff to watch their children while they went back to class. Though it was the staff's job to watch the children, the mothers still had to take responsibility and make sure the staff was willing to watch them.

Community College

That evening, the girls without restrictions went on a ride through the city of Cleveland. The others left the young light-skinned girl and me with the staff and the babies. I sat in the recreation room with Ms. Viola and the two small children watching Barney. Clevetta, the young finger sucker that was never formally introduced to me was on restriction and had to stay in her room. I didn't go because I had to earn points on Euphrasia's levels system. Earning higher levels made it permissible to access Euphrasia's activities and privileges. I didn't want to sit and watch the children watch TV, so I went to my room.

Euphrasia's evening schedule was like Scioto's: shower by 6:30 AM; breakfast by seven; school by 8 AM; twenty minutes of free time before our 12 pm lunch; dinner by 6 PM; and in bed by 8 pm. The best part about Euphrasia was the bedroom doors didn't lock behind me and I didn't have to knock or ask permission to go to the bathroom. The only setback was that I couldn't use the telephone as much.

I stuck a piece of tape on the back of a picture of myself and hung it up. I sorted through my pictures and came across one of Jacob and myself at the prom. Prom was another reason the Magistrate probably sentenced me. When prom came around, I was on house arrest. I told my mom not to call the Magistrate to get permission because she'd probably deny my request. I was going to the prom regardless; after all, it was a school event. I didn't want my mom to call because I didn't want to take the chance of the Magistrate telling me no. Although the Magistrate said I couldn't go to the prom, I went anyway.

I stared at myself in the picture. The maroon fitted spaghetti string dress had little gold sparkles, a heart shaped neckline, and a sexy slit that went a little higher than my knees. My mother and I shopped all over the city until we found the perfect dress. My shoes were my favorite part of my attire. I wore gold high heel sandals with clear heels. I referred to those shoes as my Cinderella shoes.

I had fuchsia-colored extensions glued in and styled with Shirley Temple curls and a swooped bang. Finally, I got a full balance with a new set of nails. Jacob accompanied me to the prom wearing a black double-breasted suit with a gold vest. We were sharp together.

There was a school located on the first floor of Euphrasia's building with only one classroom and one teacher. The inmates described the inside of the joint, as being on the ins, and referred to the outside world, as the outs. Pregnant girls from the outs also attended this school. I was upset that Euphrasia's staff expected me to go to school. I finished my first week at Euphrasia sitting and looking out the window, doodling names I wanted my baby to have. I didn't see any reason to participate because, although I didn't walk the stage, I earned my high school diploma and was a high school graduate. I didn't know what the staff at Euphrasia expected me to do, but I wasn't planning on sitting through high school and participating in anything elementary.

The teacher of the school tried to encourage and challenge me to challenge myself, but I wasn't feeling her. She thought it would be better if Euphrasia got permission to send me to Cuyahoga Community College which was a few blocks down the street. In the meantime, the teacher gave me permission to write letters to my friends. She wanted me to stay busy and said she didn't have anything else for me to do besides assigning me to read a book.

The first week at Euphrasia went by as slowly as the last three months had. The letters I received from my mother twice a week were sincerely heartfelt, and she never missed a Saturday visit. It meant the world that my mother supported me one hundred percent. Jail is a lonely place. Every book about jail describes the same lonely feeling. Letters from people I wanted to hear from were rare, and the people that supported me weren't the people I expected to.

I had one friend Merriam who accompanied my mother on the two-hour drive from Columbus to Cleveland. She made the trip twice to see me for no more than five minutes. I appreciated all four hours she sacrificed to come and see me. When I called Merriam's house, her mother also proved to be compassionate and a great supporter. She'd place me on hold to call Merriam and her sister to the phone, no matter how long it took them to come. I'd hear her through the receiver screaming both of their names.

Many of my closest friends had a hard time finding time to write or support me. Ava's mom put a block on their phone which hurt my feelings, especially knowing that Ava accepted calls from some of her boyfriends that were locked up. Additionally, for the most part, I only called with a calling card provided by and paid for by my mother. I knew my friends were having the time of their lives enjoying their first summer out of school as adults. I knew my friends couldn't push the pause button for me. I was sure they'd moved on with their lives. Being in jail is like dying; the world goes on with or without you.

Later that day, I had a meeting with the therapist assigned to me. Her office was located on the same side as the other unit. I walked into the office with my spitting cup in my hand and sat down. This was my first-time meeting Ms. Norah.

"Hi Keturah, I'm Norah and I'll be your therapist while you're here at Euphrasia."

I didn't say anything, I just stared at her. I didn't have anything to add. I put my cup to my mouth, hacked up some mucus, and spat. Ms. Norah looked at me with her face and nose turned up.

"That's nasty, I know you don't have to do that, do you?" she said in a sadity, stuck-up kind of way.

I stared at the dark, skinned woman. She had smooth dark skin, beautiful silky long black hair, and a big gap between her front two teeth. I gave her the same ugly look she gave me.

"Yeah."

"I don't know if I'm going to be able to stomach that," the young pretty plump woman said as she gifted me another nasty look.

I put the cup up to my mouth and spat again. I could tell this made the woman nauseous, but I didn't care. The woman had a job to do and I didn't care if she did her job or not. I didn't want to talk to her anyway, especially about my personal business.

Ms. Norah went over my treatment plan, which I worked on while at Euphrasia. She handed me a packet of levels, which explained and described the activities I'd be working on. She also said that within the next two weeks, I'd be enrolling in Cuyahoga Community College. I'd gotten my wish after all; I'd be starting college in the fall, as I'd always dreamed.

For the next week or so, I sat in my unit and played with the children. While Daytona was in school, her three-year-old son attended Head Start at a center down the street. She had her son when she was thirteen, and to my surprise, she'd been in Euphrasia twice. Her mother kept her son the first time they locked her up. The second time, she was fortunate enough to have her son at Euphrasia with her.

Clevetta literally lived in the projects next to Euphrasia. Clevetta's son was fortunate because he went to her aunt's apartment since they lived so close. Living close was also convenient because she went on more home visits than the rest of us girls. Sometimes when we went on walks around the neighborhood, we'd walk past her apartment.

I didn't think Euphrasia was that bad of a place to finish my time. I didn't like the fact that most of the staff was at most, five years my senior. I couldn't stand them telling me what to do. I made sure, I did everything I was supposed to do before anyone had a chance to tell me anything. I didn't give them any reason to say nothing to me. I just figured I'd avoid any friction that might come my way.

Some of the girls had to play nice with the staff. Being in jail was a hassle that made beggars out of some of the girls. Some referred to it as hustling, but most girls at Euphrasia hustled the staff for their essential needs. My mother brought me everything I needed and was permitted to have. I didn't think I needed anyone else during my time at Euphrasia. I couldn't bring myself to kiss anyone's butt; I had too much pride. I didn't believe the staff liked me much because of that, and I didn't care.

12 CAGED BIRDS CAN SING

On Friday and Saturday evenings, I felt privileged getting out to get fresh air. At the same time, I thought the van rides around the city were kind of insulting. It was ridiculous; especially since I owed my own ride. I was 18 years old, going on van rides for Saturday entertainment. In hindsight though, those rides are some of my best memories at Euphrasia. The van rides gave us a chance to forget about being in jail, gave us a chance to bond, and team build.

Some of my favorite times were going skating, swimming, and driving around Cleveland singing with all the girls along with Nas on the radio. "If I ruled the world (Imagine that)" That song was like an old Negro spiritual. I could tell that all the girls loved that song, as I'm certain, we could all relate to the lyrics. Nas' words and his calm voice ran through my blood and carried energy like no other. That song held a special place in my heart. If I ruled the world - was my go-to song when I wanted to feel free. The lyrics described how I wished it went down when I was sentenced, how I intended to parent my child, how the system should work, and gave me hope of how life could be if I lived in a perfect utopia. These ideas made sense to me.

Sometimes the other girls and I created our own utopia; we had our own rap concert in our unit. One evening, we were playing around, and someone started spitting some lyrics. For some reason, they doubted my skills, until one of the girls did the robot move and tapped me in. I laid these lines on them:

> I get wicked
> and I gets wild
> Niggas try to freak me
> like I'm a black and mild
> because I'm that nigga
> who will give your ass a head rush
> and while I'm Blazing
> ashes to ashes

dust to dust.
so bluntly speaking, nigga
you can't fuck with me
always strapped
rolling deep with my posse.
Cause…
I kicks it, I kicks it,
my lyrics, explicit
my rhymes more complex,
having deep thoughts who's next —
to roll another spliff up,
take a puff
and now I don't give a fuck.
and now I'm seeing double,
take another hit
and now I'm in for trouble —
traveling to a holy place,
my chronic high,
thinking to myself is there a
ghetto heaven in the sky.
I smokes the chronic,
but only the heavyweight killer-
pass the blunt —
so I can take a puff, my nigga.

#

Losing privileges of any kind in life can feel like taking two steps backward. Every time I stepped outside of Euphrasia's doors, I thought about my freedom. Walking out those doors reminded me of how important my freedom is. On the other hand, especially in jail, losing privileges and being on restriction was a debilitating and discouraging experience.

I tried so hard to be perfect, to keep my mouth shut, and to mind my own business; but, sometimes outside forces and the challenges that came with them defeated me. On the bright side of things, at least it wasn't Euphrasia's protocol to strip all privileges away at once. If we were restricted from leaving Euphrasia, the next best activity to spend points on was the radio.

Radio time could be just as liberating as the van rides. Most times, we spent our radio time alone in our rooms with the door shut. I'd close my eyes and let the music take me back to whatever place the music represented. Musicians are some of the greatest poets. I had a mental block and for a while I couldn't create poetry. I couldn't be in the same moment with my pain. It was too depressing to think about and I didn't own my true feelings at the time. To write great poetry, I had to be in my feelings.

One of my favorite rappers of all time, Tupac Shakur and his song "Dear Mama" also articulated and captured exactly what I felt. His song did more than speak to me, his music consoled me. None of my close friends could relate to my experience on a personal level, but I knew Tupac could. I related to him because just as his mother was in jail when she was pregnant with him, I was in jail pregnant with my daughter. When I heard "Dear Mama" the words resonated as it perfectly described the respect that I had for my mother and what I felt when I was sentenced. This song touched me emotionally, and I often cried listening to it. I knew my experience was not unique. This song made me feel like I could make a comeback from my situation. He and his mother were an inspiration to me.

Historians usually ask older folks where they were when icons like John F. Kennedy or Martin Luther King Junior died. For Generation Xers, Tupac was our JFK/Martin Luther King Junior moment. When people ask me where I was when Tupac died, I always have a quick answer.

The night Tupac died, Clevetta had radio time and heard the DJ broadcast the horrific news of his death. She ran out of her room crying and announced Tupac was dead. It was unbelievable. It felt so much like a family member died. His death hit me hard, and I mourned for him and my freedom that he represented.

Community and Territory

Natalie was on our unit the longest. She was 17 and the oldest girl there before I got there. She didn't make it a secret when she claimed her own shower. When we only had four people in our unit, I followed suit claiming my shower, and a toilet too. I cleaned my toilet and slid my tube socks onto the toilet seat to let everyone know, that was my toilet, and no one was to use it; especially, the girls from the other unit.

When a new girl arrived on our unit, Natie and I laid down the rules that there was only one other shower left to use and the other girls had no choice but to share it. One day, Natie used an interesting form of persuasion to stop the new white girl from using her shower. She told the white girl that because her shower nozzle sprays the hardest, white people can't handle it, because it would cause bruises on their skin. No one ever knew what might come out Natie's mouth.

Learning how to live in a community, especially in that setting was challenging for me, like Natie, I found it necessary to lay down a few rules. One morning I watched as Daytona poured some alcohol in the cap, dipped a q-tip in the cap, and cleaned her son's ears or whatever was infected, and, at one point, double-dipped the q-tip in the cap. Daytona poured the contaminated alcohol back into the alcohol bottle and placed it back in the community cabinet where the rest of our personal effects were kept. I observed and was mortified. "You might as well put your name on that," I said with my face most likely scrunched up.

"What?" she said defensively.

"You put all your baby's germs in that bottle."

"It's alcohol Keturah, it cleans itself," Daytona said.

"Well, I can't use that."

"Daytona, Keturah's right, you shouldn't have poured the used alcohol back into the bottle," Ms. Viola inserted herself into the conversation settling the debate.

"My son doesn't have no diseases!" Daytona defended her philosophy.

"That's not the point Daytona! There's no need for getting offended. Put your name on the bottle and that alcohol will only be used for you and your son."

#

Sometimes, the staff felt inclusive of the community. Occasionally, they found ways to bond with the girls. In public, we were all protective of one another. One time we went to an outside pool located in one of Cleveland's hoods. It was a hot beautiful day, and nothing could've ruined our free time. As we walked in the pool area, all the local patrons stared at our diverse group as we were happily minding our own business. A hood-rat chick blurted out, "Look at those ragamuffins." The small group that surrounded the rowdy girl erupted in laughter.

Miss Tammy chimed in and warned the locals "Don't let their looks fool you. Fuck with these girls if you want to, but they are all felons; so, you've been warned!"

Miss Tammy's comment silenced the small group's laughter and our group continued to have a wonderful time at the pool. We were outside the doors of Euphrasia and doing regular activities that free people did; we weren't bothered at all.

#

I received a letter from my mother that read:

Sept 6, 1996

Hi Keturah, how are you feeling? Keturah, I'm about to tell you something that is important, and you need to do everything I tell you. Keturah, regardless of how justified you feel because you were only defending yourself, you need to focus on your priorities now. Your main goal is to get out of there. You need to stop telling those people that you were defending yourself and take responsibility for stabbing the girl because the courts feel different and it's in their hands now.

We both know that the Lord knows the truth. When those people start questioning you on how you feel, you need to tell them exactly what they want to hear. Like, I know I was wrong to cut the girl. And I am sorry that I did. If I could relive it again, I would've walked away because being locked up is not worth it and they're still out going on with their lives. Next, say I wish I would've left; this will make them feel and believe that you understand what you did and that you know it was wrong.

Wake up! What you truly believe and feel, don't matter! You must give them what they want and say what they want to hear. Stop what you're saying because we know what happened, but the counselors must write a report to the Judge as well, so, you need to start telling those folks exactly what they want to hear. You don't have long to go, and in November when you go in front of the Judge, you want all the reports to be positive – you don't want negative reports made about you. I told you this last week, listen and do what I'm telling you!

Tell those folks regardless, if you mean it or not, tell them what they want to hear. White folks don't care anything about us black folks, that's why so many blacks are in jail. Keturah, you got to, and I mean as soon as I tell you or you read this letter, start telling them what they want to hear. Well, it's late and I'm going to bed. Miss you, but I don't miss that spitting, thinking about it makes me a little sick.

Love you,
Mom

#

My mom sent me that letter giving me scripts to use and urged me to take responsibility for my actions. No matter how I felt about the circumstances, she was right, I wasn't helping my case by continuing to deny that I was wrong for stabbing Boomquifa. I guess that was the major reason the Magistrate denied my early release. It's hard to write something or say something I don't believe. My mother raised me to be honest, and I found it hard to tell a lie. The truth didn't help keep me out of jail, but now I wasn't only looking out for my best interest but was also looking out for my unborn child.

13. BIRTH OF MY LITTLE ANGEL

I opened my eyes and grabbed the spit cup that was next to me. I laid in the dark with my eyes wide open. I felt small contractions. The first ten minutes into labor, my intuition told me it was real labor pains. I wanted to alert the staff but first wanted to be positive that I was in labor. In between the contractions, I walked the four corners of my room stopping to look out the window at the streetlight that lit my room.

For two hours, I paced my room before my contractions became consistent. I turned my light on and opened my door. The night staff sat at her post in a chair in the middle of the hallway. Ms. Agnes sat there in her usual position, slouched down in her chair with her arms and legs crossed. Ms. Agnes looked more like a bull-dagger. She always wore jogging pants and an ugly shirt that didn't compliment her shape. She had a short curly haircut and wore old fashion eyeglasses. She looked and acted weird. That woman was a strange one.

"Ms. Agnes, I think I'm in labor." I gripped the pillow that I held and squeezed it tightly. Gripping the pillow helped me quiet my moans.

I explained that I'd been up for two hours and my contractions were five minutes apart. Ms. Agnes explained that she was also required to monitor my contractions for an hour before she could give the nurse a call. I didn't think I'd ever get to the hospital. I called my mother and Jacob and told them I was in labor and would be heading to the hospital in about an hour.

Miss Tammy and I walked out of the doors and Cleveland's cold wind smacked parts of my exposed face. I looked like a hog in my blue First Down bubble coat – I had managed to gain all my weight back, along with 15 extra pounds. I had a matching hat and gloves on too. I watched my feet as I walked through the fresh dusty snow. I took a big step into the big brown van and sat in the front seat. I only got that privilege when I went to the doctor for a check-up. I tried to silently endure the pain; the same way I handled the horrible jail spirits that constantly attacked me. I was screaming on the inside, as the contractions struck like lightning.

When we arrived at the hospital, everything went smoothly. They quickly got my room ready; and when the doctor checked my cervix, he said, I'd only dilated two centimeters, so he told me to walk around the hospital. By 6 o'clock in the morning, I was so hungry. I'd never heard that labor gave women an appetite, but I was starving. I went back to my room and called the nurse to request something to eat. The nurse explained that the only way I could eat was if I went back to Euphrasia because the doctor didn't know how long I would be in labor.

I chose to go back to Euphrasia to eat. Miss Tammy and I made it back by 9:30 AM. By the time, I made it to my unit and sat down at the dining table, my pain climaxed, and I realized I'd made the wrong decision. It wasn't a good idea going back to Euphrasia. It was Sunday and all the girls on the unit were cleaning. I was waiting in the dining room for Miss Tammy to come back with my plate from the hospital kitchen.

My stomach was tight and hard as a rock; and, I could hardly move. No one noticed me and I couldn't get anyone's attention. I struggled and barely made it to my room where I laid bent over on the floor. The contractions came fast, one after another. While lying there in a fetal position, I held my stomach and hummed. Clevetta opened my door, saw me crunched over on the floor, and quickly ran to get the staff. Ms. Viola came to my room, looked at me, and alerted Ms. Norah of my urgent need to go back to the hospital.

With the help of the staff, I got back on my feet and half bundled up. Ms. Viola put her arm around me and chanted, "Breathe through your nose and out your mouth." I didn't want my coat zipped up because I didn't want anything tight around my stomach and waist. I pushed Ms. Viola's arm away, I was irritated, frustrated, and didn't want anyone touching me. I thought at this moment that I'd be scared, but I wasn't. I wanted my labor to be over and I just wanted to get the baby out of me.

The only problem was someone had the brown van, so our only option was to take the white van, which had no shocks. Ms. Norah and Ms. Viola drove me to the hospital in a hurry. We must've driven over every bump and pothole in the city. Every bump brought on a stronger contraction. I thought I might deliver in the van.

When I arrived back at the hospital, the nurse instructed me to sit in a wheelchair so they could push me to the maternity ward. Sitting wasn't an option, and that's what I told the nurse. The nurse politely went over the hospital policies and explained she couldn't take me to my room unless I sat down in the wheelchair. I eased down in the chair and kicked off my shoes. One shoe flew behind the registration desk and I'm not sure where the other one landed.

Sharp pains waved and traveled in a spiral motion, starting at my lower back, down to my thighs. The excruciating pain repeated itself. A petite, female nurse came and measured my cervix. I'd dilated 10 cm already. The nurse introduced a male student nurse, a big-tall man with blond hair; he looked like a Russian man. The nurse asked permission for him to check my cervix too. I wanted them to get the show on the road. I agreed. The male nurse stuck three fingers in, and I jumped back. I gave him a definite look of death. My facial expression told him all he needed to know. He got the message that he'd need to practice on someone else.

At the same time, another nurse came in to administer my IV - my mother, Phil and Jacob arrived. I looked down at the puddle of blood that dripped on the sheets. The nurse missed my vein and my arm imploded with the fluid from the IV. Everything and everyone moved swiftly. My back pain intensified. Every time Jacob touched me; excruciating pulses traveled through my body. I turned on my right side. I didn't want him touching me. Was this pain a punishment?

My mom massaged my back, up twice and down twice, totaling four rubs. "We're going to smoke," my mom told me. I was happy my mother and Jacob moved out of the way. I moaned loudly as my pain amplified and accelerated. Jacob watched in horror.

I thank God for sending me some on-time angels. A volunteer midwife massaged my lower back. Ms. Norah massaged my upper back. The pain rippled from the bottom of my thighs up to the middle of my back in deep constant waves. Every wave felt like thin razors cutting through my back and thighs.

My room was chaotic. Jacob, Ms. Norah, Ms. Viola, and a couple of nurses surrounded my bed. The doctor came and directed the nurse to clear the room. Ms. Norah and Ms. Viola looked at each other and refused to leave on the grounds of me being an inmate. The baby was coming fast. The doctor, nor I, had time to debate with either of them. Ms. Norah was very helpful and provided me the support that a sister would provide to a sister. I appreciated her support.

The nurse draped me with a disposable cover. She grabbed a long crochet hook. While the nurse broke my water, Jacob grabbed my hand and squeezed it. The warm water that dripped down my butt was soothing, but only for a moment, then the pain increased.

The blood and watery liquid flowed from my womb and out of my vagina. Jacob staggered. A nurse held him up until his legs were back under his control.

My stomach tightened. I wanted the baby out of me. My plan was to have a natural birth, however, the pain persuaded me to ask for some relief.

"Would you like an epidural?" the doctor offered. Then, the doctor quickly withdrew the offer after he looked at my cervix. "It's too late to give you anything; the baby's coming too fast!"

That meant I'd have my baby naturally. I felt a force of pressure. I grunted loudly. It was hard to interpret the confusing signals coming from my body. I didn't know if I had to vomit or poop. I grunted again. "I got to doo-doo!" I yelled.

"Try not to push," a nurse, said calmly.

The volunteer continued to rub my back in a circular motion. I appreciated the woman rubbing my back. Ms. Norah backed up so the professionals could do their job. Jacob glared.

"Uhhh!" I pushed.

"Don't push until I tell you to!" the nurse coached me.

I followed directions. And I breathed.

"Not yet!" the doctor said.

I pushed anyway. I couldn't help it. I pushed three times. The baby's head popped out. The doctor suctioned her nose and mouth.

"Keturah, we got to get the baby's shoulders out now." I listened closely to what the doctor was saying. "Push now!" the doctor said. He assisted the baby and her broad shoulders as she shimmied out of my vagina; The doctor cut the umbilical cord and rested my baby on the warmer, then suctioned her mouth and nose some more. Jacob walked over to the baby and looked over his first-born. The nurse bundled the baby up and put the baby in his arms.

"What about me, I'm in pain," I moaned. Everyone forget about me and I instantly became invisible after the delivery of my daughter. The nurse walked over, placed a silver bowl underneath my butt, and began to massage my abdomen. Two minutes later, I delivered the afterbirth.

In my arms, Jacob placed our baby, who looked more like an angel than a baby. Because my daughter made a bowel movement in my stomach, as a precaution the doctor put her on antibiotics, which she'd have to take for seven days, just in case she swallowed some of the fluid. One nurse advocated for me to stay at the hospital to breastfeed, and more importantly, bond with my baby. She insisted and tried to persuade the director of Euphrasia to allow me to stay with my baby for the week, but they denied the nurses' request.

A couple of hours later, we could visit our daughter in the intensive care unit. We looked in the incubators for the names of the babies. I saw a baby that was barely a baby at all. The baby looked to be in her sixth trimester of development. I thank God my baby came out a healthy six lbs., three oz., and twenty-one inches. I had a baby girl with a head full of hair, except for a small ball spot on the top of her head. My'Angel was a beautiful golden-brown baby.

Jacob found our baby, and I walked up and stood by his side. The two of us looked at our baby amazed that we'd created something so real. I was amazed someone came into this world through me. I became a one-way portal into this world. I named my daughter My'Angel for obvious reasons.

I didn't want my visitors to leave. Having my family around liberated me. Once visiting hours ended, I went back to ICU to be close to my baby. I didn't ever want to leave her alone. I hadn't rested since I had her and still found myself excited to get to know my little angel.

14 GRANDMA

So many of my childhood experiences resurfaced with the birth of my motherhood. I had to sort out all the things I knew about being a mother, the good and bad things. The famous Psychologist Eric Erickson explains that people try out roles to learn who they are and who they want to be. I carefully thought of the women that influenced my motherhood. The obvious people like my mother, grandmother, three aunts, many of my teachers, and many other motherly figures; as well as, characters of the 80s T.V. shows. All of these women presented me with ideas and scripts that ultimately helped me to choose the best attributes from these women to formulate the kind of mother that I wanted to become, my own slice of pound cake.

Besides the rape incident, for the most part, I appreciated my mother and her parenting skills. But that one incident ruptured our circle of trust, which at times, I believed we'd never repair. I was confused about motherhood; being a good mother and failing to protect my little angel was my newest and greatest fear. I feared what happed to me, would happen to her.

My maternal family is the greatest influence of my motherhood. Hands down, my grandmother was a warrior and the ultimate superwoman. Now, nobody could ever compete with her, for this woman was close to Jesus. My grandmother was born in 1933 in Columbus, Ohio, during the worse year of the depression. My grandmother was a beautiful, virtuous, strong, honest, courageous, wise black woman; and nevertheless, many people misunderstood her strength and motherhood. Not many knew that she was a sensitive woman because her strength hid her vulnerable nature and attributes.

She quit school in the 12th grade and explained that her white teachers only gave her two choices; she could take sewing, or cooking classes. She stated she wanted to be a professional woman with a professional career, so she quit school. Throughout her life, she worked as a Chef for a popular hotel. My grandfather and I used to drop her off at work before the sun rose. I loved to ride down Route 161 and look out the windows at the fluorescent lights on the busy route that we routinely took to drop my grandmother off.

It was special because sometimes she'd cook us breakfast at her job. After she got hurt on the job, she retired. The routine of dropping my grandmother off in the morning when the breeze was cool and it was still dark outside, welcomed a new day to start. Early mornings are still special to me because of her. These memories, I've captured, stored, and can still recall to this day; along with the fluorescent lights of Route 161.

My grandmother started having children at 18. She and my grandfather never became empty nesters in my grandmother's lifetime. She sacrificed over fifty years being the sole caretaker and surrogate mother to myself, many of my cousins, and over the years, would pitch in with her great-grandchildren.

My lips could never utter a sore word about her, for she was the Great Oz behind the curtain, but she was no phony. She was the truth. My family is a matriarchal family and my grandmother was the disciplinarian, most likely, not by choice. Due to my grandfather's passive ways, my grandmother was unfairly misunderstood. She loved all her children uniquely. My grandmother didn't take stuff from anybody. She respected you and you were going to respect her.

My grandmother loved to cook and was one of the best. Her role in the family was of great importance. She ran the household, was the accountant, took care of all the finances, paid the bills, did the grocery shopping, and rationed my grandfather his weekly allowance out her brassiere. My grandmother made most of the household decisions. She also knew how to survive in this world filled with racist and sexist agendas, which society magnified throughout her living days.

For the first two years or so of my life, my mother and I lived with my grandparents. My first memories are of their home. When I was no more than three, I remember my cousin going off to school, me helping bring in the milk and cheese WIC dropped off and left on the front porch, and me cleaning the house with my grandmother. That's when I thought cleaning was fun. The older I got; the more cleaning turned into work. My grandmother taught all of us children many lessons we'd later appreciate - like keeping a clean house, washing dishes, sweeping, vacuuming, mopping, dusting, wiping the cabinets, wiping out the microwave, cleaning out the refrigerator, picking greens, cleaning chitterlings; and making the boys plates, amongst many other things. My grandmother understood, what only mothers understand - these things don't clean themselves. After being corrected or chastised by my grandmother, my cousins and I frequently declared we were never going back to my grandparent's house. A week later, we'd begged grandma to have us back for a weekend.

The crickets and birds singing outside as my eyes peer through a small hole, as I threaded a needle for my grandmother, are warm happy memories. When her eyes became too old to focus on the small hole of the needle, I understood it was my responsibility to thread the needle. Spending time with my grandmother was special. She and I both loved black and white films. My grandmother especially loved to watch love pictures, which is what she called them. I'd stay up all night with her, sleeping in between her and my grandfather. And when I outgrew my welcome sleeping with them, she or Granddad would make me a pallet on the floor.

Although I have such fond memories of her, I couldn't decipher her pound cake until after I became a mother. I didn't understand all involved with motherhood and parenting. In my lifetime, I've had the privilege to be at the bedsides of two dying people. One of those people was my grandmother. It's heart-wrenching to witness someone sacrifice their entire life and not receive in life the appreciation and admiration they deserved.

It's hard to be the backbone, and easier to become the scapegoat when seeds don't bloom or over bloom. The environment is crucial; whether it's nature versus nurture or a combination. Seeds need soil, water, sun, and a little attention, which all equals love. But the mother of the seeds can never predict all the storms the seeds may live through. Her duty is to provide the seeds with just enough for them to be healthy and thrive on their own. Sometimes, it's not that the seeds lack receiving water, but watering the seeds abundantly, causes the seeds to rot.

Now, take the seeds for instance. Its job is to receive the water, the sun, and share the soil with its mother. But sometimes, the seeds outgrow the mother, and the mother is dribbled and eventually drained dry until there's nothing left. My grandmother sacrificed her time and her life, but that made her happy.

Parents often improve themselves to give their children a better life. My grandparents enjoyed caring for their grandchildren despite having to sacrifice their entire lives. Some people often become mean and resentful when they realize their life is passing by and they've been left with someone else's responsibilities. There aren't many people that desire or find pleasure in this great sacrifice. My grandmother loved being a mother, grandmother, and great-grandmother. Unfortunately, and more sadly, when my grandmother died, she still questioned whether she over or under watered her seeds. I'm thankful though, she had the great ability to love her seeds despite the type of fruit they produced. That is where I found her recipe for pound cake.

#

From the women in my family, I've learned many attributes; some I'll adopt, and others I'll urgently divorce. My priority is to consider the best interest of my child. I won't abandon my child for any reason. I will sacrifice my life for my child. I am humbled to earn the trust of my child. I am eager to participate in the life of my child. I will focus on balancing how and what I nourish within my child. I vowed to live by this affirmation, just as my grandmother did; but, with some adjustments and discipline, so both my daughter and I can thrive in this uncertain world.

I looked at my baby and wished I could hug her. I longed for the day to come when my daughter and I could breathe freely without permission; together we'll have our first breath of freedom. Before heading back to my room for the night, I talked to her through the incubator until I could no longer hold my eyes open. I slept peacefully all night long. While admitted to the hospital for 48 hours after I gave birth, the staff gave me all the personal space I needed; and I appreciated their kindness. Being able to go as I pleased; meant I was able to visit my daughter in ICU as much as I wanted.

Ms. Norah made a sincere effort it approved for me to stay at the hospital with my daughter, but the Ohio Department of Youth Services denied my request. I was in jail and the State didn't see breastfeeding or mother-daughter bonding as a special reason to extend any privileges. I was a prisoner and O.D.Y.S. treated me like one. Having a baby in the juvenile system was one of my punishments and being at Euphrasia was the privilege. I was a product of the pipeline to prison. Now my womb was an extension to that pipeline, and I hoped to break that cycle for my daughter's sake.

My Aunt Harriet tried to break our family cycle of unwed motherhood by making a deal with each of her nieces. She wanted to make sure none of her nieces made the same mistakes that she and her sisters made. She promised to take those of us that walked the stage without a fetus stain in our womb, on a trip out of the country. I obviously failed to live up to her standards and expectations. I did, however, consider her proposal when I contemplated abortion. My mom reassured me the trip was now irrelevant because getting pregnant was a pregnancy. My mother's honest, unpretentious nature kept mine in check. The trip didn't matter, I was happy to be a mother.

The next morning, around 9 o'clock, the hospital moved my daughter out of ICU. A nurse brought her to me and taught me how to breast-feed. My daughter and I had an instant connection. She latched onto my breast with knowing instincts.

My body still ached with pain from the back labor, and I could barely stand straight. Surprisingly, the spitting had eased, almost disappearing. I couldn't win for losing though, when things seemed to improve, something else happened to counter the positivity. I was having a hard time dealing with the fact that by evening, I had to leave my baby in the hospital for the remaining five days to complete her treatment and return to Euphrasia.

I was terrified. I'm not a doctor nor did one diagnose me, but I was sure I was already suffering from separation anxiety. How could I leave my daughter alone and protect my child at the same time? God made me face another situation that stripped me of my dignity and experience as a first-time mother. The system proved to be a powerful dehumanizer.

If I had to bite my tongue one more time, I thought I might bite it in half. I was proof the system worked, putting people in their place in society, not only a literal place but also a mental place. Jail demeaned and dehumanized my value, dignity, and violently pierced parts of my soul. There was no way; I was walking away from that place as the same person. I felt raped again by the demoralizing experience.

Under the circumstances, I had no choice but to swallow my heart and leave my baby at the hospital. Before I left, I fed her, kissed her, and promised I'd be back early in the morning to see her. The nurse took the bottles filled with my breast milk and assured me she'd take good care of my daughter.

The next morning, I woke up bright and early, excited to go see my daughter. I informed the staff when I was ready. Ms. Tara was a large sweet woman, a little on the ditzy side. She called to the other unit for my escort to the hospital. The other staff told her there was a staff shortage because someone called off work and another staff member were running late. I tried to be patient but eventually lost my cool. I wanted to scream, but of course, I couldn't. A half-hour passed and I finally lost my temper. Euphrasia finally got to see my pent-up rage explode.

"Where's my ride at? I want to see my baby!" I demanded as I paced up and down the hallway like a mother lioness. I erupted like hot lava flowing from a volcano. I finally had a good reason to scream. "I want to see my baby!" I screamed and began to wail at the same time. "Somebody take me to see my baby!" I demanded loudly.

I was tired of playing the role of the goody-two-shoes; it hadn't gotten me anywhere so far. I was a mother now. I just wanted to see my baby. Overnight, I must've developed my mommy balls. I didn't shut up until I got my way. I was frustrated and upset. I didn't hold in my feelings. They heard me loud and clear, and it felt good too. People needed to hear me, and they did.

Ms. Molly walked through the big gray doors, her face was glowing red. She stopped where I was sliding down the wall, hugging myself in a cradled position with my eyes red and puffy.

"Now you look here, I don't know what's gotten into you, but this isn't the way you get what you want. Now, this will get you a ride back to Scioto to finish the remainder of your time, and we'll send your baby home. You wouldn't get to see her at all."

I considered her words before replying. With tears streaming down my face, I stated, "Yawl said I get to see my baby and I want to see my baby!"

Ms. Molly didn't say much more because she knew I was speaking from my heart and hadn't been a problem since the time I arrived. She knew my request was sincere.

"Be patient. In about an hour, we'll have enough staff to cover both units and we'll take you to the hospital. I would be disappointed if you get in trouble over this. We'll drop you off and you'll be there until 5 o'clock. You'll get to see your baby every day, but we must follow the rules. Since we can trust you to walk to and from the college, we believe that we can trust you to go to the hospital to fulfill your duties as a mother. If you act like this, you won't get anywhere here or in life. Do you understand?"

"Yes," I answered.

Ms. Molly confirming that I'd get to see my daughter made me feel a little better. I felt like life was trying to tear a wedge between my daughter and me, as it had caused a split between my mother and me; and, I wasn't going to allow that. Ms. Molly was telling the truth. It wasn't the first time someone told me I needed to change my attitude, if I wanted to get somewhere in life. My experience with punishments, particularly, my incarceration was a constant reminder of how I should move through life.

One time, when my grandmother sent me outside to get a switch for my spanking, I thought I was being smart and brought back an old dried-out stick that crumbled almost to the touch. It would break into pieces upon the impact of my legs and behind. My grandmother was so furious she sent me back outside to get a flimsy switch with the thin endings; the kind that makes the swiping sound when swung back-and-forth like a fan. I got extra swipes for trying to pull that stunt.

Jail made me realize what she meant when she said, "You like to do things the hard way!" What she meant was because she'd already had such experiences, like Jesus, she'd sacrificed and suffered through the experiences and by sharing it with me, was her way of saving me from personally having experiences that might be avoided.

#

For five days, each morning, the staff dropped me off to the hospital and picked me up by 5:00 PM. On October 20, the hospital released my baby to me. I saw it as an early birthday gift from God.

That same day, I received two cards from my Aunt Harriet. One was a birthday card and the other card filled with words of inspiration.

The outside of the birthday card read:

For a niece who's very special to me.

The inside read:

Throughout the days and years gone by, I've watched you change and grow, and now that it's your birthday, I just wanted you to know that, through all of your birthdays, it always has been true, I've been so very glad to have a special niece like you. Happy birthday!

Love,
Your Aunt and Uncle

The second card had a picture of Martin Luther King Junior on the front of the card. MLK was standing with a microphone in front of him delivering a speech to a crowd.

The front of the card read:

Especially for you, a message of inspiration by Martin Luther King Junior.

I opened the card and on the left side, it read:

When the history books are written and future generations, the historians will have to pause and say, "There lived a great people that are black people – who injected new meaning in dignity into the vase of civilization," this is our challenge and our overwhelming responsibility. Martin Luther King Junior.

The right side of the card said:

Take pride in who you are and never stop reaching for all you can be.

My aunt wrote below it:

Keturah, I just wanted to give you a gift of inspiration. Because of your current situation – and you're having a baby, things will be more difficult. That's a given. However, always remember, life is what you make it. If you want to succeed, you will. Don't ever doubt yourself. People now expect you to fail. But I'm certain you will prove them wrong. "Go on and do great things!" P.S. I have faith in you and your abilities,

Love you,
Aunt Harriet

15 LOSING IT

When you're in jail for some reason, gossip from the outside travels fast. If someone wants you to know something while you're in jail, he or she will find a way for you to get the information. I learned from a source that Jacob was driving a blue car, and he didn't own a blue car. I had my suspicions he was seeing other people and I expected him to. But he hurt me. He was self-proclaiming his love and loyalty, but still lying to me.

When he showed up to visitation with remnants of glitter on his face, my gut told me he'd been to the Ohio State Fair with a girl and had obviously been close enough to rub up against her. That was enough for me to consider breaking up with him. Ms. Norah warned me in a session of how unrealistic it was to believe our relationship would last. I received a letter from my mom about her concerns as well.

My mom learned through Ms. Susan, Jacob and his mother were trying to get custody of my daughter. Neither, he nor his mother had ever communicated any interest in raising my daughter; so, this infuriated me. I couldn't trust him or his mother. I felt violated. I didn't understand how he could betray me like that. But I wouldn't play the fool, I had me and my daughter's best interest in the frontlines of my mind and in my heart.

#

I didn't know how long I'd get away with staying on the unit with my baby, until, Ms. Molly made it clear the gap between the break and the start of a new semester was too far apart. Maternity leave at Euphrasia meant no cleaning, no gym, and a pass to sleep in the middle of the day. I didn't do much of any chores before I gave birth at any of the facilities.

I witnessed how female inmates' natural caregiving instincts kicked in. It's evident in the way they cared for me. However, after maternity leave, I became like the other girls and was required to partake in performing chores. Ms. Molly told me I couldn't stay on the unit and do nothing. She explained that my only options were to get a job or go to school with the other girls.

I didn't want to leave my baby, but I figured it would be nice to save some money to take home once released. Ms. Molly gave me a few days to think about my choices. If I decided to get a job, I could choose from one of the three fast-food restaurants around the corner from Euphrasia.

At the end of my six-week maternity leave, I went to work at Burger King. I worked four to five hours a day. I used to work at Burger King before, which was the first place I'd ever worked. I liked working and being around real people from the outside, free people. Working made the jail experience more bearable.

I felt human walking to and from work. I felt like part of the community. My coworkers reminded me that I was human. When I worked the fries, the heat stimulated my breasts and they'd fill up with milk. Hearing other children cry also stimulated them. On many occasions, my breasts leaked through two or three breast pads. I'd walk around with two big wet spots on my shirt until a co-worker put my breasts on blast and pointed out the wet circles.

I carried my breast pump to work with me and pumped on my breaks. Phil had three baby showers for me, and his friends and co-workers bought everything I needed for my new baby, down from the breast pump, a crib, baby clothing, bottles, blankets, a diaper dispenser, and diapers. My coach sent me a beautiful baby blanket and a baby book. Although I've had some traumatic life experiences, I've always felt God's angels around protecting me.

There were too many rules at Euphrasia though, I breastfed for many reasons besides the obvious health reasons. Breastfeeding was my excuse to sleep next to my daughter and the excuse I used to avoid write-ups. It was against the rules to sleep with our babies because of the danger it poses. I also decided to breastfeed so I could control when and how much my daughter ate. I didn't like how the staff controlled and monitored how the girls fed their babies. Some of the staff made assessments I didn't believe they were qualified to make. Some of the staff crossed boundaries and force-fed their personal culture, values, and beliefs onto most of the girls.

#

I applied for an early release twice before, but each request was denied. Having the ability to apply for an early release provided a form of hope in prison. It's something I looked forward to, to mark a date on the calendar, and a reason to believe that the Judge would one day, grant my early release request.

I was desperate for an early release. I was so desperate; I begged Phil and he'd make three-way calls so I could speak to psychics. All I wanted to know was when the Judge was going to release me. I got so mad at God I stopped praying. Some girls attended church on Sundays just to have something to do and to get out of Euphrasia, but not me.

I couldn't bring myself to pray or enter His house. I mean, he couldn't have been listening to me unless he too was denying all my requests. At first, I didn't take my treatment all that serious. Of course, "They couldn't help me." I didn't need God, and I didn't need their help. I'd already been through counseling after the rape. But eventually, I faced myself, looked in that mirror, and humbled myself. I realized my mother was right, I had to take responsibility for stabbing Boomquifa.

Chicken

Monday morning Ms. Molly came and spoke to Natie, Daytona, and me about the complaints she received from the other girls. They were jealous because they couldn't get a job or get to eat fast food. Nobody wanted the burgers from Burger King, but I always found it worthwhile waiting for Natie or Daytona to bring back Kentucky Fried Chicken. Ms. Molly informed us that she could no longer allow us to bring food back to Euphrasia.

Ms. Molly couldn't stop us though. Natie and Daytona smuggled in the chicken in their pockets. I'd go in my bathroom stall, sit down on my socks, and slam on the chicken, then wrap the bones in a bundle of toilet paper, and dispose of the bundle by placing it at the bottom of the trashcan. Interestingly, after Ms. Molly forbid us from bringing food back to Euphrasia, it became more desirable.

#

I received a letter from my mother that read:

October 28, 1996

How are you and my grandbaby doing? I know she misses me already :-). Keturah when you come home, you need to take care of a few things. First, you need to file for custody. Right now, you and Jacob both have custody. That means he can take the baby without your consent and he doesn't have to give her back.
That's what happened to Sheila's friend – plus you need to apply for child support. You got to look out for what might happen down the road. Jacob and his mother are being supportive now, but you never know, so look out for you and the baby. His mother will probably get mad, but hey, like she's looking out for her son, I'm looking out for my daughter. Keturah, you must do all of this when you come home. I wanted to tell you this Saturday but we had Grandma and Granddad over for company, but they would have agreed because they made me file for child support with you and your sister; and that's one time I was glad I listened.
    Love you,
    Mom

#

I hadn't thought about or considered applying for child support. I didn't expect to get pregnant and Jacob didn't expect me to get pregnant, it's just something that happened. We both used free will when we created My'Angel; I assumed she would be our priority, and that we both would focus on her. I wrestled with the idea of putting Jacob on child support. I wanted to be fair; I wanted to be a good friend too. I didn't know what to do, but my mom's advice was probably the best advice.

I spoke to some of the other girls to see if they planned to put their child's father on child support. All the girls had different perspectives. I'm not sure how much of it depended on the status of their relationship. Having a child out of wedlock puts stress on both the father and the mother. I had to consider all of my options. Are the two of us friends? Were we in a relationship? At the end of the day, we didn't have future plans. These were important questions to consider. I understood different levels of co-parenting could make life challenging. Being an unwed parent, I considered two important legal issues which affected my life and our child's life forever; child support and custody were only the tips of the iceberg.

My mother was right; I couldn't let my heart get in the way of making a logical decision. Friendship was irrelevant whether we were friends or not, we still had to be co-parents to our daughter. After I watched my grandmother, mother, and aunts over the years, I knew that parenting is a business. Running a household is a business. Going to work or working is a business. Going back to school is a business. Kid's having extracurricular activities is a business too. These are only some of the things, I envisioned myself juggling as a parent. I decided to follow my mother's advice.

#

I received another card from my cheerleading advisor which had a big red heart on the front cover, centered perfectly in the middle of the card. The writing read, "I have you in my heart. At the bottom of that heart, there was a scripture: Philippians 1:7." She had written on both sides of the card and a handwritten letter was included.

My cheerleading advisor wrote:

12-17-96

Dear Keturah,

I was happy to hear from you the other day. I had just called Phil to find out what was going on – I knew you were going to see the Judge on November 13, but I didn't know what happened. I'm sorry to hear that they did not grant your early release – it must've been hard to hear that you had to stay because you were doing well! – That does not seem fair or just – but I do believe that everything happens for a reason, so we will have to be patient and find out what that reason is.

How is your little girl - I'm sure she is beautiful like her mother! I'm anxious to see a picture of her :-) I just moved last week so I am including my new address and phone number – I'm finally buying a place, so now I will not have to rent anymore.

I have been busy trying to unpack and still get my Christmas stuff done. Last night, I baked three kinds of cookies and two kinds of bread. I didn't get to make my gingerbread men like usual but there will be time for that again next year. On Saturday, I leave for Texas to see my parents. It will be a two-day drive, which can be extremely boring, but I brought some of those books on tape to listen to during my drive.

I hope that you are doing well, though you were not able to go home. What a wonderful Christmas present to have a little baby to spend it with. Sometimes, it makes me sad to know that my students are all having children before me - but someday I will have my own; and by then, yours will be old enough to babysit!

Take care of yourself and your little girl. Keep your chin up - Christmas will be over soon and you will not feel as lonely. January and February are slow months anyway (not much to do), hopefully, the Judge will release you.

When they release you, I would love to have you come visit me! We'll go out and celebrate your release. Write to me soon and let me know how you are doing. I will be gone from the 21st through the 31st, but I think you will hear from me again.

With love,
Ms. Myers

#

My emotions were still a roller coaster wreck and I couldn't stop thinking about getting out. Every day when I woke up, I crossed off another day on my homemade calendar. Unless you've gone to jail before, you would never imagine how many times an inmate looks at the calendar. I was homesick and more than ready to go home. Jacob wanted our daughter to accompany him to West Virginia to visit his family. I hated the thought of my two-month-old baby, crossing state lines without me; but I agreed if he dropped our daughter to my mother on the agreed-upon day.

In addition, I received a letter from Jacob's mother wishing me and My'Angel a merry Christmas. She explained that she sent us a Christmas ornament and a card. She also stated that she was going to West Virginia for Christmas to celebrate her 40th birthday and trying fake fingernails for the first time. Her letter was short, sweet, and demonstrated thoughtfulness. At least, that's what I initially thought.

Christmas Day

On Christmas Day, I didn't talk. I cried because Christmas was always a special time of year for my family. It was my mother's favorite holiday and she always made it special. She always made sure I had the best Christmases. She'd have beautiful decorations all over the house, lots of artificial snow covering the Christmas tree, and many gifts under the tree. She'd play Nat King Cole's Christmas album to create those special moments. I could always tell that she loved to see the smile on my face while opening the gifts; me smiling ear to ear seemed to make her smile from ear to ear too.

My mother said she didn't put a Christmas tree up. She promised we'd go shopping when I got out. I didn't care about the gifts; I just wanted to be with my family. This year, I'd miss my grandfather's pound cake.

Everyone thought I was a buzz kill. I walked around with a long face on Christmas Eve. My face was long as my first day incarcerated.

"Why don't you change your face up?" Natie asked.

"For what, this year, I'm pretending Christmas ain't coming; makes it easier for me to get through this season; there's nothing for me to be excited about. I'm just happy my baby's too young to remember her first Christmas."

The generous staff looked out for all the babies. All four kids had several gifts under the tree. I was pleasantly surprised that we all had a few gifts wrapped with pretty bows.

Ms. Maddie, an older black woman, who looked like a pro-black activist, especially when she wore African printed dresses. She had the qualities to bake pound cake, there was no question about it. The well-dressed woman carried herself in a way that exemplified a serious loving auntie, better respect me air about her – the type that would talk to you in a calm voice and make you cry. All the girls respected her. She catered a Christmas dinner with her own money, and boy was it a treat! She brought in collard greens, rolls, turkey, mac & cheese, potato salad, sweet potato pie, a cake, and lots of love.

Her gesture was genuine, thoughtful, and priceless. That home-cooked meal turned my entire day around. We all slammed and filled our bellies. She didn't bring a pound cake, but she certainly made all her food with love.

My'Angel Goes On a Journey

The snow fell heavily from the dark navy-blue color almost black sky. I had an overwhelming feeling of helplessness. I spoke to my mother and she hadn't heard from Jacob, he was more than twelve hours late.

I couldn't leave to find my baby. I couldn't call my mother as much as I wanted to check on my daughter. I was powerless. My skin itched with anxiety. The first night, I stayed up all night, staring out of my bedroom window taking inventory of each car that passed. I hoped and prayed my child's father would pull up with my baby.

"That's the kind of car, but not the color. That's the color, but not the car. Where could they be? Why was I so stupid? That's the car, but not the color." I was anxious and delirious. I stood in the window for hours looking at every car that rode down the street. I beat myself up with my thoughts each time a car passed.

The second day, Ms. Viola said I couldn't use the phone to check on my baby because I neglected to get the address, phone number, and whereabouts of her in the first place. My anger exploded. Her comment made me furious. As I walked out of the room, I picked up a small chair and threw it through the office door. I'd lost it. The screams that I tightly encapsulated in my being were released. And although I felt bad, it felt good. I received my first write-up that day. The staff claimed I almost hit one of the babies on the unit. I was placed on restriction, which didn't help my cause.

The staff was just as pissed as I was because they were responsible for both my daughter and me. They called the highway patrol to make sure no accidents had occurred from Cleveland to West Virginia. My therapist planned to file a missing person's report the next day.

Sunday came and went. Jacob never dropped our baby off to my mom, nor did he have the decency to call me. He didn't show up until Tuesday morning. For three and a half days, I had no idea of the whereabouts of my baby. I only knew he and my daughter were traveling to West Virginia. I had no clue, as to what part. I felt so irresponsible. The universe was testing my motherhood. The fact that I overlooked getting emergency contact information pertaining to my daughter's whereabouts made me question my motherhood as well.

The doorbell rang and I ran to my room to look out the window. I saw Jacob's mother's minivan parked in the front of the building. I peeked through the crack of the grey security doors and waited for the staff to escort me downstairs to get my baby.

Jacob stood there with my baby in his arms as if everything was hunky-dory. I looked at him and wished he could read my thoughts.

"You're a dumb ass," I said as I snatched my baby and her bag out of his hands and told him not to worry about coming to get her again.

"Quit trippin', the weather was bad, and we weren't able to travel through West Virginia," he said pitifully.

"That's exactly why you should've called me. I guess you or your mom couldn't get to a phone. You and your mother are so inconsiderate. You take my two-month-old baby out of town, you didn't call me, or let me know where my child is for three days...you should've called me or my mother to let us know what was going on."

I was so angry and didn't want to hear any more of his excuses. I had My 'Angel back and I was happy about that. We skipped the happy goodbye that day and the kiss we used to sneak. I didn't waste any time having Jacob removed from my visitation list. Ms. Molly and Ms. Norah also banned him from taking our daughter overnight.

16 JAILED BIRDS CAN FLY

Jail manipulated time in such a manner that each second was like a frozen Iceberg, melting and drifting slowly. I felt the force, which weighed me down forcing me to reflect on my past. I took a deep look in the stone-cold waters. Imagine watching a movie and only seeing one frame of the scene and being incapable of fast-forwarding the moments. Imagine watching this non-changing scene every day, with the same characters, saying and doing the same things, over, and over again. I wanted to fast-forward my life to the day of my release.

I became quite fond of Ms. Norah despite the nasty faces she gave me when I was pregnant, although my spitting drove her crazy and she forced me to look at her disgusted scrunched up face. By the end of my sentence, I believed Ms. Norah understood me.

Sitting in therapy one day, Ms. Norah asked me, "Keturah, honestly answer one question for me?" I looked at her uncertain. "How come you don't tell Phil that you love him when he tells you that he loves you?" Ms. Norah must've struck a nerve because tears streamed down my face. She walked over and put her arm around me. "Do you want to talk about it?"

"No," I erupted with tears and sadness. Ms. Norah had gotten too personal. My mom's rules regarding her personal business staying in our house had played out in full over the past few months. Ms. Norah attempted to talk about my feelings about my mom and Phil, my biological dad, and the stabbing of my neighbor. I still wasn't comfortable talking about my feelings, I didn't know how to begin to truly own them.

"I just don't say I love you; he knows what I mean," I said as if I made my point clear.

"Please elaborate because there's more to it than, I just don't say it," Ms. Norah said.

"I don't say it, my mother doesn't say it, nor does my grandmother. My grandmother says it's not my mom's fault that she doesn't say it to me. My grandmother once explained that I shouldn't blame my mother for not telling me that she loves me. My grandmother and grandfather didn't say those words to their children."

I didn't know why Ms. Norah had made this such a big deal. This was all I knew; this was normal to my family. "We're not the huggy, kissy type of family," I reiterated.

"Well, if I told somebody I loved them, I would want them to return the love with more than, you too. Do you tell your daughter that you love her?" Ms. Norah asked looking at me.

"Of course, I do," I looked at Ms. Norah, her face still trying to win me over. "I tell my daughter several times a day, every day. I can't stop saying it if I tried."

"If you told your daughter that you loved her, wouldn't you want to hear her reply, I love you too?"

"Yes," I wanted to smirk because I understood whole-heartedly and got her point. I agreed, hearing it out loud sounded and felt good, and it would hurt my feelings if I sent out words and admirations that weren't returned. I guess it does make a difference.

Sometimes people need clarity. I needed my mother to clarify our relationship. I wanted my mother to tell me that she loved me. I promised myself, I'd tell my daughter that I loved her every day.

#

After my daughter was born, she cried all night. I had the doctor check her over because I thought she had colic. I firmly believed that during my pregnancy, I transferred my negative energy and emotions to her. I didn't want to curse my daughter with my sins. I made a conscious decision to work harder to release my baggage. I had no choice but to change my attitude towards the world so my daughter's environment wouldn't be stressful. I wanted my child to know nothing but love, that's why I hugged and kissed her so much.

At a meeting, one staff brought it to everyone's attention that I smothered my baby by holding her all the time. Mrs. Betty suggested to Ms. Norah, to force me to put my baby in the crib. Fortunately, Ms. Norah agreed with me, Mrs. Betty had no grounds to suggest such a ridiculous recommendation.

Caring for an infant all by myself was difficult. One night, I asked the staff to watch my daughter because I was exhausted. I didn't make this request often. I didn't want anyone holding or touching her. A couple of nights had passed since I had some sleep. So, I reached out for some help.

Natie's bedroom was the first, located off the staff's office. Natie had a good view of Ms. Agnes. Natie always slept with her head closest to the door and with her bedroom door cracked. The night I asked Ms. Agnes to watch my daughter, Natie saw Ms. Agnes scratch her coochie and pick up my baby without washing her hands. Natie didn't keep this a secret either; she waited for the opportune moment to expose Ms. Agnes at a combined unit meeting.

Ms. Molly asked the group if anyone had any concerns and Natie raised her hand. As soon as she called Natie's name, Natie made more of a statement as opposed to asking a question. In her Cincinnati dialect, she said, "I want to know why Ms. Agnes was scratchin' her coochie and why she picked up Keturah's baby without washing her hands?"

All of the staff's mouths dropped open. Ms. Molly advised Natie that the combined unit meeting was not the appropriate time or place to discuss her question.

However, all the girls laughed, including me. Natie left a big smile on my face. After the meeting, Ms. Norah led the four of us mothers to our unit. She asked Natie, "Did you have to ask that question in front of the other girls?"

"Yeah, she shouldn't have scratched her coochie and held Keturah's baby without washing her hands. She's nasty," Natie answered. We all walked back to our unit in solidarity, shaking our heads in agreement.

#

Ms. Norah finally brought me some good news. The Magistrate finally granted my early release and I'd be leaving Euphrasia! I'd waited for this moment for nine and a half months. I couldn't believe my release day was coming. I saw people come and go during my time locked up. I didn't know how to act, but I had a big smile on my face. The other girls left Euphrasia hugging and kissing the staff as if they were going to miss them. But I knew that would not be me.

I was desperate to get back to my life. Things would never be the same, but I was up for the challenge. I had a couple of weeks left and I had a strong desire to taste freedom. I was already making plans. When I went home to visit, I called my old job and secured a position. I planned on starting my old job a week from my release date. I prayed for the flowers and trees to be in full bloom on the day of my release. Spring weather was an extra treat, a way for God to greet my daughter and me at the door.

Writing an apology letter to Boomquifa was the only barrier standing in between my early release and me. I had no other choice but to admit my crime and show responsibility for my actions. I didn't want to write Boomquifa a letter, but I picked up a pen to free myself. Jail taught me a lifelong lesson in the art of swallowing my pride and humbling myself.

Dear Boomquifa, I'm writing to you to apologize for the agony I put you and your family through. I never meant to hurt you and I sincerely hope you're well. In the last several months, I've learned to take responsibility for my actions. I would like to express how sorry I am. My sister passed away and I wouldn't want to cause you to feel the pain that my family and I feel. I hope that you can accept my apology.
Sincerely,
Keturah

#

Fear of the two sisters and their mother sharing the apology letter consumed my thoughts. I was fearful that they'd show it to everybody on the block. I was sorry but not for stabbing the girl. I was sorry because I went to jail and gave birth to my daughter inside the juvenile penal system.

#

Since my mother was unable to visit me on my last weekend there, my grandparents volunteered to. They got permission to cook and bring food and pound cake for everyone. My grandfather's pound cake always reminded me of his home; the only place, I absolutely felt safe. Eating my grandfather's pound cake placed me at his table, in his kitchen - my safe place.

Later that evening the sunny sky changed as the clouds sailed in filling the dark spaces. The trees danced in the wind and the showers poured. Each raindrop fell like little torpedoes, exploding as they hit the ground. I looked out the window and held my baby in my arms as I watched the storm cruise above Euphrasia.

The staff had a couple of movies stored away for days like this. My daughter and I joined the others in the activity room to watch my favorite movie, "The Color Purple". I loved this well-known classic in the black community mostly because I could deeply relate to several of the themes and characters. I sat in the back of the T.V. room and placed my baby's carrier next to me.

A scene in the movie placed me in the apartment of our living room with Lucifer raping me. I felt myself screaming silently and struggling underneath him. I once again felt the pain I felt the day I was raped. The cries of my eight-year-old-self crawled into my grieving abyss and released the floods of confided anguish. I glanced down at my daughter and knew God blessed me to have My'Angel at my side. I promised God that I would never allow anyone to hurt her.

Another part of the movie that choked me up was when the character lost her sister and later found her. I wished her situation, was my situation. I wished I could discover that my sister wasn't laying under the plush green grasses of Green Lawn Cemetery. I understood that when I lost my sister, I lost someone that the world could never replace. Time was a poignant antagonist, relentlessly tugging at my sanity.

I knew what the main character felt like too: to have her heart, her confidence, and her self-worth ripped from underneath her. I understood what the compassion of her protagonist meant to her. The compassion expressed was equal to my guardians; they embodied support for which I'll always be grateful. I smiled knowing that I was almost free. Life had whipped me raw and exposed layers of my emotional scars, enough to expose my truth. I only prayed to be the best mother and person I could be and hoped the world would accept that.

#

My mother was careful and strict, but she dropped the ball for a moment. It happened to be a big moment. It's hard to pretend that Lucifer didn't rape me and that my mother didn't betray me. The fact is, the rape and betrayal happened, and I can't change my past. I've dealt with this pain every day of my life.

At the end of the day, I reserve judgment. I know and understand that before I take my last breath, if I live the rest of my life in a straight line and only deviate from it once, people will only see and remember my high and low moments. These moments are the easiest seen, like the rising and setting of the sun. If one day is representative of my life, and I'm judged based on my rise and my fall; it would be more than audacious and hypocritical for others to judge me based on those two experiences.

It's easy to judge others when standing on a straight line, but I've learned to keep in mind that my highs and lows may happen in a different time zone than other peoples, which may obstruct my judgment. Before judging another, be sure to have all the evidence before casting judgment. If you don't know what you're talking about and pass unqualified judgment, you could cause another person more pain. Because I can't be omniscient and I am not perfect, who am I to judge one moment of my mother or another's life?

It took years for me to understand my mother's recipe for pound cake, because of my obscured view and because of my own dark abyss. I rarely review old letters, which powerfully reflect and capture old feelings - words people find hard to say but find the courage to write. Some things are easier written than said, especially if the love language hasn't been learned.

The day before my release, I separated the letters according to their sender, and ordered them by their dates and read all of them. I had more than a handful from my cheerleading coach, and a ton from my mother, both wrote me consistently. After reviewing my mother's letters, the content and words she used to express herself were mostly loving verbs, consistent with love, protection, encouragement, guidance, and hope. Her salutations were all signs of her expressing her love and affection for me. My mother's consistent love and support were her pound cake offering, and more importantly, her redemption.

As far as Boomquifa, it would take many years for me to realize that when I stabbed her, I stabbed myself. It would take many years for my spiritual awakening to happen. I finally got it - Boomquifa is a part of God, and I am a part of God. What I did to her, I did to myself. I imagine God as being a straight line. Since a line is infinite and has no beginning and no end, all humans are connected to God's infinite line.

Humans must be standing on a straight line. No one is in front of, behind, on top of, or beneath anyone else. Whether born in 2bc, or 1926, or the year 1977, alive or dead, we're all standing on a line that keeps us connected to God and one another. I believe every one of us can affect the stability of the line. People have a greater effect on people they're closest to, and some people impact other's they only have a brief encounter with. That's why it's important to love and care for everyone on the line.

#

I turned and looked at my bedroom. I couldn't believe the time that passed. I was anxious to get out of Cleveland and back to Columbus. Phil drove up to get my daughter and me. I walked out of Euphrasia's front door for the last time, and I prayed I would never see the inside of any jail ever again.

Jail audaciously worked on me and in return, I learned about my pain, my glory, and myself. I learned that life is ambiguous, and I was no longer able to fabricate my truth. I had a new vision for my life and a new role as a mother. I had spent ten months in jail and was happy to get on the highway. I looked up and watched the birds fly freely in the sky. These months taught me that jailed birds fly differently. They have a rough start, but they can fly.

I found something I didn't know I'd lost. I felt empowered and armed with an experience that strengthened me to hold my tongue, step outside of myself, and no matter how painful, face the challenge of looking within myself to shed old skin. Most importantly, I learned that self-control and self-discipline are essential to control my life and how I spend my time. I learned that I should create new, exciting, happy, courageous, healthy experiences to quicken experiences of daily routines, boredom, sadness, sickness, and fear.

Part of my parole and one of the biggest stipulations didn't allow me to live in my parent's house. I had to stay away from the victim and her family. Since they lived next door, I had no choice but to move in with my grandparents. I didn't complain, I was free, and my daughter was by my side.

Two in a half hours later, we pulled up to my grandparent's house. It looked brighter than it had before. My mom was waiting on the porch. I walked in the house and I felt loved by a few of my family member's comforting, energetic, warm laughter. After they left, I ate the last slice of pound cake and exhaled. I was happy! I wasn't at my house, but I was home.

ABOUT THE AUTHOR

Kenwanna is the author of Pound Cake Poetry, Monster Pew! Clean Up Your Room! and Danny's Key to Freedom. She is a writer, poet, photographer, and earring artist who loves to create.

www.ingramcontent.com/pod-product-compliance
Lightning Source LLC
Chambersburg PA
CBHW060340170426
43202CB00014B/2830